Butterfly
In the City

A Good Life
in Costa Rica

by

Jo Stuart

Illustrations by Sandra Conant Strachan

First published in 2006 by Litografía e Imprenta LIL, S.A,
Costa Rica

ISBN: 1475049013
ISBN-13: 978-1475049015

Dedication

For my sister Annetta,
for all the reasons she knows.

Acknowledgements

Most of the chapters in this book were, in one version or another, columns written for *The Tico Times* or *amcostarica.com*. I thank Dery Dyer, editor of the former, and Jay Brodell of the latter for giving me the opportunity to write about my impressions and experiences living in Costa Rica. In *The Tico Times* my columns ran under the heading, "I'll Take the City." In *amcostarica.com*, they are entitled "Living in Costa Rica."

There are two Sandys in this book, both dear friends. Sandra Conant Strachan lives in Escazú and is a talented writer and artist. It is to her I am grateful for her always thoughtful critiques of the written word, Hebrew National hotdog dinners and, most importantly, the charming illustrations she did for this book.

Sandra Shaw Homer lives in remote Tilarán, which I understand is beautiful, but I couldn't do it. She too is a writer, a bonsaist and a former fellow columnist at *The Tico Times*. It was she who responded with an enthusiastic yes to my request to serve as editor of this book. Without her dedication and gentle persistence, the chapters that follow might never have made it out of my computer.

I also wish to acknowledge my dear friend Bill White, who founded the David and Julia White Artists' Colony in Ciudad Colón. He read everything I wrote for both publications and liked everything he read. His praise and encouragement were a constant support.

And finally, I would like to thank the Costa Rican people for their part in making this book possible.

Jo Stuart
San José, Costa Rica
January, 2006

Preface

In April, 1990, I wrote the following column for Interworld News, *the newsletter of the International Center at San José State University, a residence housing students from all over the world:*

Last summer I visited Costa Rica. When I told people I was going to Costa Rica some asked, "Aren't you afraid of the guerilla warfare?"

"No, that's El Salvador."

Others wondered, "Won't the communists give you a hard time?"

"No, that's Nicaragua."

Still others said, "Ah, that island in the Caribbean?"

"No, that's Puerto Rico."

In the middle of war-torn Central America is this tiny peaceful country that abolished its army in 1949 and whose recent president had been awarded the Nobel Peace Prize. I wanted to visit such a country.

Costa Rica and its inhabitants, who call themselves Ticos, charmed me. I found myself walking around with a smile on my face. Peace seemed to be a value held by all – and not just world peace, but a peaceful way of dealing with everyone. The money saved on armaments is spent on education (there is over 90% literacy) and medical care, and there is also a real concern for the environment. Just a little country of four million people whose power to influence the world does not come from its riches or ability to threaten, but simply from its ability and desire to be a model for peace.

When I returned home to California, I couldn't help comparing the International Center, where I serve as Director, with Costa Rica. Many people are confused about who we are and where we are located. And certainly we are a small institution – only 77 students – without the resources to change the world. But we are a model of peaceful coexistence, cooperation and caring among people with different world views who value learning. I sense it every day in my exchanges with the residents: in observing their interactions, in the concern we all share for the house we live in, and in the peaceful energy that permeates the I-Center. It is probably why I felt so at home in Costa Rica when I visited there.

Two years later I moved to Costa Rica.
Since then, over the last thirteen years, I have written more or less constantly, noting down glimpses of what everyday life has been for one woman living alone in a foreign country. I was fortunate to be able to publish many of these observations, and quite a few are included here. They do not, however, appear in chronological order; rather they are organized into categories so that one can find items of interest more easily. My hope is that this volume will help others to have as easy a transition into Costa Rican life as I have had.

Table of Contents

Singing the City... 1
San José is Beautiful, No Matter What They Say.......... 3
Giving Directions... 5
There is Culture, and Then There is *Culture*............... 7
Coals to Newcastle... 9
The Pleasures of the Meseta Central...................... 12
Both Music and Water Have Charm....................... 14
The Dry Season Isn't Always Dry......................... 16
I Sing the City Eclectic..................................... 18
Where is St. Patrick When You Need Him?............... 20
The A-Mazing Central Market............................. 22
Bus-it around Town... 24
Sidewalk Cafés.. 26
Taxis – A Luxury Elsewhere, a Bargain Here............ 29
Taxista Advice.. 31
Street Smart.. 33
The Times, They are A-changing.......................... 35
The Magic of City Parks.................................... 37
Sunday in the Park.. 40
Butterflies in the City....................................... 42

Getting Comfortable in a New Culture......,,,..... 45
A Christmas Carol to Costa Rica.......................... 47
Culture Shock Happens..................................... 49
Everyone Should Have Someone at Thanksgiving........ 53
A Funny Thing Happened on the Way to the Theater..... 55
How to Think of Bus Drivers as Poets.................... 56
Costa Rican-style Marketing on Streets and Buses........ 58
Uniforms are the Mode Here............................... 60
Learning the Umbrella Ballet in San José................. 62
The Peace Corps is Alive and Well in Costa Rica........ 64
Grandma Prudence Goes to School........................ 66
Becoming a Resident Changes Your Outlook............. 68

Renewing My Residency, 2003............................. 72
The Continuing Saga of My Residency Renewal.......... 74
Still Renewing my Residency...............................,,, 76
The Transition from Tourist to Resident................... 78
Rule Number Four... 80
Tico Sayings.. 83
Parsing "To Serve" and "To Help" in Costa Rica......... 85
Pet Peeves... 88
When in Rome, First Check Things Out.................... 91

Food for Thoughts..................................;; 95
The Eternal Debate: Broccoli vs. Chocolate.............. 97
Living the Comfy Narrow Life............................. 99
Second-Hand Rose...101
Combating the Snarls...103
The Incredible Edible *Feria* Egg...........................105
More Reasons for Shopping at the *Feria*...................108
The Gourmet Get-together....................................110
Whatever Happened to *La Plume de Ma Tante?*............112
Happiness is a New Water Heater...........................113
The Joys of Dining at Home Alone.........................116
Thoughts While Making *Gnocchi Verdi*...................118

Politics Here and There................…..............121
The Cruelty of Countries.....................................123
Election Day in the Civilized "Developing World"......125
I'll Take the Potholes...128
How to Achieve a Critical Mass............................130
People Power...132
And Not a Drop to Drink Pretty Soon.....................134
Gail's Kids Now Have a Chance for a Future............136
Women on the March..138

Staying Healthy in Costa Rica......................141
Starting the New Year Hitting the Ground Running.....143

One Tough Cookie....................................145
A Patient's Dilemma.................................147
Favor de cuidar mi campo in this Endless Line........150
Side Effects and Natural Cures.....................152
Wherein our Heroine Discovers yet another Hospital...155
Unexpected Fast Times at the Clínica Duran...........157
The Many Faces of Waste............................159
The Singing Patient................................161

People, Places and Ponderings.....................165
The Joys of Living Alone...........................167
New Country, New Identity..........................169
Aggression and the Fragile Male....................171
Stepping Down as the Queen of Clutter is not Easy......173
Complacency is a Bad Idea..........................175
Normal Doesn't Live Here Anymore...................178
Cowgirls Aren't the Only Ones Who Get the Blues......180
Happy Birthday, Mom................................182
Going There vs. Getting There......................185
Halloween..187
Semana Santa with Mavis..........................189
Wedding Bells for the Two Sandys...................192
Those Tiny Things that Go *ZZZZ* in the Night...........194
A Few Cures for the Rainy Day Blues................196
More Rainy Day Blues...............................198
When it's Time to Move On..........................200
The Bottoms of my Socks............................202
Reading *The Kitchen Boy* in Escazú................204
Science Catches Up with the Past...................206
Sometimes I Think in Quotes........................208
The More Things Change, the More I Object...........210
If the World Were According to Stuart..............212
Give Me the Simple Life............................214
Of Time and Money, and Spending Both in Costa Rica.216
Unexpected Gifts...................................218

Singing the City

San José is Beautiful, No Matter What They Say

From time to time, I forget how much pleasure the city of San José gives me. I say this in the face of protests from friends who have visited me or live outside the city. I begin my defense by saying (with apologies to the Peace Corps' slogan) that San José is not the toughest, but the ugliest, city I will ever love. I do love it, and I don't really think it is ugly.

That realization was renewed recently when I found myself downtown before 9 a.m. The air was still sweet from the night's breezes; the streets were not yet absolutely jammed with people and vehicles. I have learned to spot the dangerous irregularities in the sidewalks a half-block ahead so that I can look around and enjoy myself. Having no car, I make a habit of noticing one-way and less-traveled streets, newly paved ones and shortcuts. This has earned me the reputation, a friend told me, of being the biggest backseat driver in Costa Rica. Many taxi drivers will confirm this.

This particular morning I decided to walk to the Central Market to buy some *vela* (sailfish) – an inexpensive delicacy I have recently discovered. My first smile came as I stood aside to let a Tica (Costa Ricans call themselves Ticos) walk through a narrow passage first and got a gracious *"Gracias, muy amable."* And I shared a smile with the young man at the fish stall after I complimented him for cutting the piece of fish to within five grams of my order. Actually, I smiled and he grinned with pride. I smiled again, feeling smarter than Columbus as I walked out of the market through a different door from the one I'd entered, and still knew where I was.

I then headed down (or is it up?) Avenida Central – such a pleasure now that so much of it is a pedestrian promenade. When I first arrived in Costa Rica I was walking on Avenida Central on a rainy day. I was walking in the edge of the street because I seemed to be out of step with the other umbrella-wielding pedestrians on the sidewalk. A car swerved and headed right at me. I jumped up on the curb just in time, appalled and dismayed that a Tico driver would actually try to kill me. It was only much later that I realized that he probably didn't even see me – he was just avoiding a pothole. Now I can walk along the promenade without a care, not even of a pickpocket, with all these new police people on the streets. And today, even that driver has far fewer potholes to contend with.

The many recent pedestrian-friendly improvements in downtown San José tell us *josefinos* that we are valued. The extension of the pedestrian mall in front of the Post Office is just one of them. The photographs showing the city's pride are justified. (Now if they would just reinstall the flower kiosks or give shop owners an incentive to put pots of flowers in front of their stores, we could compete with Paris!)

But in fact, San José has a noble history of thinking about its people. When the army was abolished in 1948, the fortress at Calle 17 and Avenida 2, which served as a military barracks, became obsolete. It was converted into what is now the National Museum fronted by the Plaza de la Democracia, installed by President Oscar Arias in the 80's. I have been told that Arias found homes for all the squatters who had been living where the park now exists.

When Costa Rica built the La Reforma prison complex it no longer needed the old penitentiary atop the hill just west of Barrio Amón. Under the leadership of Gloria Bejarano, wife of President Calderón, this wonderful structure that looks like a fairytale castle was turned into a children's museum and a national auditorium, which offers

Sunday morning concerts by our world-class National Symphony Orchestra.

And when they discovered that the existing airport in western San José was not large enough for international flights, the property was turned into a people's park that is a wonderful island of serenity close to the heart of the city – our Central Park, if you will.

All of these changes make me smile. And since beauty is in the eye of the beholder, and handsome is as handsome does, it is easy for me to consider San José both a beautiful and handsome city.

Giving Directions

Another new study is out. It probably cost tens of thousands of dollars to come to a conclusion I could have told them for far less: people who live in the suburbs walk less than people who live in cities and, therefore, tend to weigh more. The research was done in the United States, where many suburbs don't even have sidewalks.

I am not sure which communities surrounding San José are considered suburbs, but I have friends in Escazú, Moravia, Santa Ana and Rohrmoser, and I am quite sure they do not walk as much as I do living in the middle of the city. Especially those who have cars. I am talking about expats only. Costa Ricans walk far more than North Americans, and I would wager that European expats walk more than we do, too. They are apt to come from compact cities where walking is a feasible mode of transportation. I walked a lot in New York, but in San José, Costa Rica, I walk more than I ever did in San José, California.

I suppose, in Costa Rica, one reason you might walk more living in the city is that if you grow tired, it is easy to catch a bus or hail a taxi. In the outlying suburbs both buses and taxis are less plentiful, and even if you find a taxi, how do you explain to the *taxista* where you want to go? Few streets and roads have signs and few *taxistas* know the names anyway. You have to use landmarks, and let's face it: there are more landmarks in the city. Although I live on a street that has a name and used to have a street sign, I have to give directions to a taxi driver starting with *"de la Casa Matute Gomez."* The *Casa Matute Gomez* is a mansion on the corner of Tenth Avenue and 21st Street that once was owned by a Venezuelan dictator of that name. He is long dead. Legend has it that when he fled his country the pilot of the plane carrying him, his family, servants and worldly possessions, said there was too much weight to gain altitude so Gomez threw the maid out of the plane. I think that story is apocryphal, just to illustrate what a mean man he was. The fact is that when the whole family had finally died, the home was left to a family retainer, a former maid. She sold it, and it became a nightclub and restaurant. I had lunch there once in the garden and found it delightful, but the place soon concentrated on being a nightclub and bar for young people, and then there was a murder and the police closed it down.

That was several years ago. It is now up for sale. It is still a landmark as *Matute Gomez*. It is not unusual for landmarks that no longer exist to be used as landmarks – the Coca Cola is probably the most famous. It used to be a Coca Cola bottling plant, now long closed, but it is still used as a landmark to get you to one of the city's main bus depots.

I have become "ticafied" in that I have invented my own landmark that I give *taxistas*. When I first came to Costa Rica I opened an account with the Banco Anglo, one of the national banks here. It was a wonderful bank. They paid high interest on both my colon and dollar accounts, the tellers were nice and the bank was conveniently downtown. Then there was a scandal with millions of dollars having been embezzled by bank officers, and the bank closed. At the time many customers panicked and stood in long lines to get their money out. I had been told that national banks here insure their customers' money the same as banks do in the States so I didn't stand in line. My money was transferred to the Banco de Costa Rica, and the Banco Anglo building across from the National Theater was closed. It now houses another government agency, but it is still the *Banco Anglo* to me.

When I take a taxi to the National Theater, to ensure the *taxista* doesn't go six extra blocks to park next to the theater (they will do that), I say "*Al lado este del antiguo Banco Anglo*" (the east side of the old Anglo Bank). That way they have to turn on that street – which, incidentally, is Third Street, but I don't think any *taxista* knows that.

There is Culture, and Then There is Culture

Many people who visit Central and Latin America remark that Costa Rica lacks the rich culture of countries like Guatemala or Ecuador. They are talking, of course, about the native Indian cultures that still exist, with their different customs, colorful costumes and handicrafts. In Costa Rica one does not get a sense of the exotic or of a different world, except perhaps in the remote *campo*.

But if one talks about culture in a different sense – the culture that is intended to refine and improve the sensibilities, culture that includes the arts, such as music, painting, theater and dance – Costa Rica, specifically San José, is a treasure trove. I realized this last week. On Wednesday I attended a Women's Club meeting at the Centro Cultural Costarricense Norteamericano in Barrio Dent. The guest speaker was Manuel Arce, Cultural Director of the Center. Señor Arce explained the services

7

and programs offered at the Center, which houses the Mark Twain Library and the Eugene O'Neill Theater.

When I first moved to Costa Rica I spent many happy hours in the Mark Twain Library. There I could keep in touch with what was happening in the U.S. via the English-language magazines and newspapers. As a member, I could also check out books, videos, and tapes of books and CD's. They also have computers to access the Internet. Its restaurant has the best lemon meringue pie in the city.

Thursday night was the opening performance of the new Philharmonic Orchestra at the National Theater. It was free, as will be every performance with few exceptions. I went but arrived too late: it was sold out. I was sorry to miss the program of music from Broadway and films and popular composers. It looks as if the purpose of the orchestra – to get people interested in music – is working.

Friday morning I attended a free performance of a jazz quintet in the Eugene O'Neill Theater. The group, from the University of Northern Iowa, was going to perform again that evening. Not only were they fine musicians, they composed most of their own music. The Center sponsors a series of programs of visiting artists of dance, music and theater for the price of a movie ticket. Phone 2207-7574 for the schedule of events.

Saturday night I was off to Escazú and the Blanche Brown Theater where the Little Theatre Group of Costa Rica was performing "You're a Good Man Charlie Brown." This is a musical version of the comic strip with the characters (all of them delightful) portraying the range of human temperaments from the pitiful and phlegmatic Charlie Brown to his bipolar peripatetic dog Snoopy.

Sunday morning I was at the National Theater again – this time in plenty of time – to enjoy the National Symphony Orchestra's concert of Tchaikovsky, Schumann and Berlioz, the first two pieces featuring the cellist Maria Tchaikovskaya. Concerts at the National Theater are on Friday nights at 8:30 and Sunday mornings at 10:30.

For anyone so inclined, the entire weekend can be taken up with cultural activities. And during the week there are many movie houses that show current films in English with Spanish subtitles, as well as the Sala Garbo, our art film theater. There are more than a half dozen theaters that present plays in Spanish. And besides the Costa Rican Art Museum and the Children's Museum (that wonderful fairy-tale castle that used to be a prison), there are a number of art galleries in downtown San José. And I am touching just the tip of the iceberg. If you peruse the calendar sections of the local newspapers, you will discover an impressive array of events.

What is so wonderful for me is that I am able to AFFORD all of these cultural events. My weekend of entertainment (not counting transportation) cost only ¢4000 ($10.00).

Coals to Newcastle

My friend Grady is back in town. I asked him if it was miserable flying and going through security. He said no, but when he returned to the States the last time the Customs officer was taken aback when he found dozens of packets of peanuts in his suitcase.

"You're bringing peanuts back to the States?" he asked suspiciously.

Grady informed him that you could not get lemon-flavored salted peanuts or chili-flavored peanuts in the States. That got us to talking about other things that people take back to their countries from Costa Rica (aside from the typical souvenirs, of course).

On my early trips back and forth between here and the States I would bring all kinds of things to Costa Rica— seasoned rice vinegar, chocolate chips, Feta cheese, shoes—things like that. Now Costa Rica has most of these things – albeit expensive chocolate chips and locally made Feta cheese. But there are shoe stores in every block. I remember once saying that when I could find herring in sour cream here I would become a resident. I found herring in sour cream in Little Israel in Pavas (and I am officially a resident).

Now, like Grady, I find myself taking things *to* the States. One time I saw a woman filling her supermarket cart with bottles of vanilla. It is not pure vanilla, although you can buy that in the Central Market. I asked her if she did a lot of baking. She said, no, her friends in Germany loved the vanilla here so she always took back a supply.

Grady knows someone who takes back 16-ounce tubs of Axion soap. He claims it is the best detergent for washing dishes and other things. I agree and have thought about taking some back to my sister, who always has a little dish of soapy water in her sink for quick washing up.

Of course, lots of people take back coffee, not just the Britt coffee for export. Britt is very good, although expensive by Costa Rican standards. Some people go to First Avenue behind the Central Market and buy freshly roasted Volio coffee to take home. It is not gift-wrapped; it comes in brown paper bags. It is cheap and good.

Of course, everyone takes Salsa Lizano back. Salsa Lizano is like Worcestershire Sauce, except spicier and cheaper. Mavis told me her son Rick took several bottles back to his home in Corning, New York, then discovered the local grocery store carried it!

I always go back with several boxes of Gallito's Milan mint-filled chocolates. My daughter, like me, has become addicted to them. In my opinion they are the best chocolates in Costa Rica for the money (aside from my fudge sauce, of course).

I used to take cans of Sardimar smoked tuna when they had the large cans in boxes. Since they have reduced the size and they no longer contain filets, I don't find it nearly as good – not worth carrying back to the States. I emailed the company lamenting this and got a quick answer from the General Manager, who told me that soon the large cans would be available in the United States. He thought this would please me. It didn't. It reminded me of one of the problems with globalization and free trade. All the best products from a country are exported and local prices go up.

Back in the 60s when I moved to Florida from New York I was dismayed to discover that the fruit in the supermarkets wasn't nearly as good as what I got in New York. And I was in citrus country! Then I noticed the fruit was getting better. I learned that the Governor of Florida had decreed that some of the prize fruit should be sold in the state. Not because of me and other residents, but because the tourists were complaining. When I first came to Costa Rica fish and seafood were very reasonable. Now shrimp is outrageously expensive here – most of it is being exported. The way the world operates now, if you have lots of money and live in one of the world's big cities, you can get the best of anything from anywhere for a price.

Some years ago there was a truck strike in California and the tomato growers couldn't get their tomatoes to the canneries. They didn't want them to rot so they sold them locally, some in farmers' markets and some to the people who came directly to their farms and picked them themselves. Customers got some good tomatoes and the farmers discovered they made more money and had more fun selling directly to the people than they did loading their tomatoes on trucks.

11

There should be a clause in all these free trade agreements that a country must keep ten percent of whatever product it exports for its own people – at local prices.

The Pleasures of the Meseta Central

When George called me on Sunday to ask if I would be interested in taking part in some picture-taking on a coffee plantation, I said yes. George works for a travel agency specializing in nature tours, and they are doing a new brochure extolling the Meseta Central's attractions. Also called the Central Valley, the Meseta Central is the area surrounding San José where the majority of Costa Ricans live. It is a series of valleys among rolling hills, peppered with small towns, villages and farms.

My job was simply to be in some of the pictures that professional nature and wildlife photographer Kevin Schafer would be taking. Not having been out of the city in a while, I looked forward to the excursion. I also think the Central Valley's attractions should be seen and appreciated by more visitors. After all, when you think about it, a view from a beach (if you are facing the ocean) is about the same wherever you are. The vistas in the Central Valley change with every curve in the highway. Highway? Make that winding, gravel, maybe tarred, narrow road.

George picked me up at 7:30 and we went to his office, Horizontes, near Paseo Colón, to join his co-worker, Jessica. Because his little SUV was overheating, he asked Jessica if we could go in her car. Since her car was being fixed, she had her dad's very big SUV, which made for a far more comfortable drive.

Jessica was going to be the coffee picker. She is 21 years old, an overachiever, lovely to look at and a delight to talk to. She is bilingual in English and Spanish and learned

Portuguese because her father went to Brazil and she bet him she could learn it faster than he. She has a degree in hotel management and is studying business administration before going into marketing. She can quote more Shakespeare than I can.

We drove to the Hotel Xanadu where Kevin and his wife Marty, with niece and nephew, were waiting. Then off we went in two SUVs in search of coffee to photograph. That part turned out to be elusive. When we stopped at a coffee plantation to pick up a guide we learned that most of the coffee had already been harvested. It ripens in December and January. Coffee has been growing in the Meseta Central since before 1800, starting with an Arabica blend first grown in Saudi Arabia. The Central Valley has near-perfect soil and climate conditions for growing coffee.

Our search for the perfect coffee plant involved much stopping and alighting from our vehicles. I got proficient at climbing in and out of an SUV (the doors are a good two and a half feet off the ground). During our stops, while Kevin was professionally eyeing the views, I learned a little about him and Marty. Theirs is one of those rare and heartwarming love stories of two people who had contentedly given up any hope of finding that perfect partner when they met fourteen years ago. Marty was the editor of a wildlife magazine and Kevin, she said, was the first photographer she'd met who didn't talk about himself. They are both avid naturalists.

We never did find a plant with more than a few red beans; Jessica didn't get a chance to play the coffee picker, nor I the tourist observing her. I posed looking at a few blossoms, but still it was a lovely mini-holiday for me, getting out of the city, breathing the clean country air, enjoying the drive through some incredible scenery (George is an excellent driver so I didn't have to instruct him from the back seat). And, as happens with many vacations, large and small, it finally was the people I met who made it most memorable.

Both Music and Water Have Charm

Wanting to write about the Calderón Guardia emergency hospital that recently opened, I went over to the old emergency room, which was closed, and asked directions from the men in the ambulance that was still parked there. I have been a rather frequent visitor of that emergency room and have great appreciation and admiration overall for the health system in this country.

I know that when the debate about health coverage rages in the U.S., someone always brings up the two words "socialized medicine!" From the tone of voice, I half-expect the speaker to be holding a cross in front of him for protection. What we have here in Costa Rica may be called socialized medicine, but it is better than the alternative that a lot of people experience in the States.

But getting to visit the new emergency facilities beyond the waiting room was not to be. They gave me the runaround. Actually I had to run around two long blocks to the office of Dirección Médico. There I was told I had to write a note to the director and wait for him to call me. So I am waiting. When I went back, without an invitation, I found the outside of the new building nicely painted yellow, green, tan and brown. Inside, this color scheme continues with a bit of hospital green here and there. The waiting room is larger and better lighted than the old one and has the required snack bar with espresso machine and soft drinks, as well as plenty of unhealthy snacks. There are two waiting areas here – the larger one is for people waiting for prescriptions dispensed from a window labeled *farmacia*. All prescriptions are free, as is a visit to the emergency room. The number of people waiting for prescriptions made me wonder if the whole world is over-medicated.

On Tuesday I was once again on the road, this time to the La Paz Waterfall Gardens. I was with most of the same happy crew of last week with the addition of Darrylle, who tore himself away from a busy day at the office. Once you have descended a considerable distance via steps, paths and bridges, you are surrounded by water in just about all of its forms – from huge to tiny waterfalls, gentle streams, and bubbling brooks, roiling cataracts, and drops of water seeping from the rocks. The air is filled with mist that freely hydrates the skin. You have to appreciate the importance of water to life and health.

On Wednesday morning, I attended a free concert at the Centro Cultural. A pianist from Russia and a singer from Maryland. There were only two of us in the audience but the two of them gave us a top performance. I was reminded of the scene in *Cabaret* that opens with a close-up of Liza Minnelli on stage in the nightclub singing her heart out. The camera pans back to reveal her audience: one lone sleeping drunk at a table. The rest of the place is empty. Watching the two performers and remembering that scene, I realized that people who are gifted with a talent, even a talent that should be shared, would be wise to learn to enjoy performing to an audience of one – themselves.

The music the pianist played, a piece by Debussy, was for me a continuation of the experience of the day before. Her fingers disappeared in a blur of movement, so quickly that the notes were like drops of water coming together to make waterfalls and rapids, bubbling brooks and seas. The soprano sang her notes purely with no seeming effort. I was as refreshed from the music as I had been from the water. Both are healing to the soul and the body. I left the concert with neither a desire nor or a need to visit a hospital, under any circumstances, for a long, long time.

The Dry Season Isn't Always Dry

On Monday, as we prepared to walk downtown, Bonnie asked, "Should we take our umbrellas?"

I hesitated. This is a trick question along the lines of, "Shall I take a jacket?" There's no way to be right, but I replied, "Oh no, this is summer and the rains have stopped." My houseguests, Bonnie and Arnold, had arrived from the States late the night before and we were getting a late start after a late breakfast. The sun was shining and it was beautiful out.

After stopping at the ATM so that I could change some money for them, we hopped on a bus downtown. I had learned that I could pay my RACSA bill at the *farmacia* right across the street from the Social Security building where my bus stops. Every day life here gets more convenient for me. Up until now, I have had to go to the ICE building on Avenida 5, which is out of the way.

Although there are a number of restaurants around the Paseo Colón and new ones opening in Barrio Dent, I could not think of one new or different restaurant where we could get a late lunch. Bonnie remembered the Hacienda from years ago when they lived here, so we walked to Seventh St. to discover the Hacienda had disappeared. I told them of the delicious *corvina* dish I had had at the Magnolia Restaurant in the Colonial Casino so we headed there. Down the block I saw the Japanese restaurant *Do*, and said, "Well, we have a choice." They decided to try Japanese. As we walked toward the restaurant, Arnold noted, "It's beginning to rain." I dismissed it as a bit of *pelo de gato* (cat's hair, the term used here for a slight spritz of rain).

16

Once settled in the clean spare restaurant, I watched as my companions chatted with the waitress, getting her input on just about every dish and finding out about her life. I wished I had that easy affability. Outside it began to rain. Really rain. Who is doing this to me, I wondered? My last guest from the States was greeted with unseasonably cold weather; now we were getting rain during the dry season.

Finally we finished lunch, chatted with the manager, had some chocolate cake we had bought in a bakery, and it was still raining. We decided to run to the Netcafe a block and a half away so Bonnie could check her email. There is a lot of buildings downtown with overhangs that come in very handy when it rains and you don't have an umbrella. We scuttled along trying to find protection but still managed to get soaked. I kept worrying that I would slip and fall, or catch pneumonia and end up in the hospital for the rest of their visit. While Bonnie checked her email, Arnold and I watched the street flood and the buses and taxis send sprays of water on unlucky pedestrians. I mentally commiserated with a young woman looking more and more forlorn as she hailed taxi after occupied taxi.

We didn't have a chance of getting a taxi home. Finally, when the downpour had settled into a harmless sprinkle, we walked the six blocks to the bus stop. Once home, we changed into warm clothing, feeling cozy again. I didn't feel that I was going to come down with pneumonia, but I did feel I needed to apologize for my adopted country's not behaving as it should. Before I could, Arnold remarked, "That was certainly a nice adventure." Just as I was thinking his spunky remark had let me off the hook, the lights went out.

I Sing the City Eclectic

I recently read a review of a book praising the industrial charms of Pittsburgh, Pennsylvania. The title of Laurie Graham's book is *Singing the City*. I didn't want to steal that, so I borrowed from Walt Whitman for my title. If someone can find enough delights in Pittsburgh to fill a book, I figure I can write a column about the things I like about San José.

Like all cities, San José has many conveniences that don't exist in small towns or the country. Cities are our cultural and entertainment centers. And San José has the wonderful Teatro Nacional in the heart of the city, where one can hear and see our great national orchestra. Also downtown is the Teatro Melico Salazar, where even the cheap seats have a good view of the stage. In Los Yoses, not far from downtown, the Centro Cultural is coming into its own with a variety of programs featuring intercultural talent at reasonable prices in its Eugene O'Neill Theater. It also has art exhibits.

Art is alive and well in many galleries in the city. If it is museums you want, we have them, too. From the Jade to the Gold to the anthropological/historical Museo Nacional in the Bellavista Fortress that formerly housed soldiers—all downtown.

My friends in small towns often lament the lack of variety in their markets. Cities are where you'll find the greatest choice of products. San José has a good sprinkling of supermarkets where fresh foods from all over the country are available, as well as imports. And it has an increasing number of restaurants with cuisines from all over the world.

And did I mention that we in the city don't seem to get the brunt of storms that flood the countryside? The streets are designed to drain the water quickly (if not for pedestrians who have to jump over the gutters). When there is a storm or other disruptive occurrence, the city is seldom without electricity for any length of time.

People who live in San José often love the very things that tourists find off-putting. In the Los Angeles airport, waiting for my flight back to Costa Rica, I talked with a woman who recently moved here. She lives in Grecia and rarely comes into the city. She said she found it scary and overwhelming. I have heard this from other expats and even locals from small towns. They add that it is dirty. Actually it is just a different kind of dirt. On the other hand, I am aware of the wonderful energy I feel from the people in the city. There is variety in this city; and in San José one can enjoy an infinite variety of faces. It is the city where foreigners from all over the world first come (unless they are forewarned tourists who make a point to avoid it).

However, there is the complaint that the city is dangerous. I cannot counter this with denial or proof that it is not. Over the years it has become more dangerous, because once most of the crime was petty – pickpockets and unarmed muggers. I remember the first murderer I read about was a man who stabbed the thief who was trying to pick his pocket. His defense was that he was infuriated that someone should try to rob him. That was then. Now we have car-jackings and kidnappings (not all in the city) and senseless murders added to robberies. But where in the world is it safer? A friend and I were wondering about this. President Bush says it is a safer, more peaceful world. Yet the number of places U.S. citizens are told not to go is growing. People seem to be more fearful and more hostile. San José has changed, too. But it is my city and, somehow, the dangers I know are easier to handle than those I don't.

19

Where is St. Patrick when You Need Him?

Some time ago, there was an article in *The Tico Times* about a snake in downtown San José. Since this was a rare occurrence it made the news. Reading about it reminded me of the first and only time my mother came to visit me here. No, no, I adore my mother. In the middle of the Great Depression, she was left a widow with four children under ten to support, and she did just that. She is smart, funny and no-nonsense. So I was thrilled when, a couple of years ago, my nephew, who was bringing a scuba diving group down here, suggested that my mother accompany them. At age eighty-six she got her first passport and down she came.

The first day she was here, she asked me if she was going to see any snakes. She was, she told me, terrified of them and had read that Costa Rica had many snakes, most of them poisonous. As far as I know, snakes and deep water are the only two things my mother is afraid of. I concurred that Costa Rica has snakes, but I assured her, "This is the city, Mom, and we may see some potholes and bumps in the sidewalk – they are always good for keeping us nimble – but there are no snakes in the city. In the jungle, yes, in rainforests, and you might find an occasional snake in the grass (little joke), but never in the city. Trust me." (I have since learned never to trust anyone who says, "Trust me.")

It was Easter week so not much was happening in San José, but I had heard about an apartment for rent and asked my mother if she would go with me to look at it. She agreed, and amazed me by walking the eight blocks to what was going to be my next apartment.

After viewing the apartment and agreeing that it was very nice, we headed back home. I dawdled in order to admire the façade of my future home, so she was about twenty feet ahead of me. I turned to see her suddenly stop. She was standing very still and looking at something in the street in front of her. I caught up.

"What is that?" she demanded, pointing a couple of feet in front of her. The tone of her voice made me feel ten years old again. (How do mothers DO that?)

I looked at where she was pointing. There it was: a slim, bright green little snake only about fifteen inches long, but coiled and ready for action and, with its alligator-shaped head raised, it looked very confident in spite of its size. It had reason to be. It looked venomous to me.

"Well," I said, in my most grown-up authoritative voice. "That is a snake." I made a big show of peering closer. "Yes, that certainly is a snake."

"What is it doing in the city?" My mother asked in the tone of voice she used to use when she asked something like, "What do you think you're doing up at this hour?"

What indeed! In all of my time in Costa Rica I have NEVER seen a snake, not in the city, not in the jungle, not even in the gra—well, maybe in the grass.

"Maybe it's looking for an apartment?" I suggested.

"Well, you better hope it's not yours," my mother shot back. "So, now what should we do?"

I took her hand and led her to the other side of the street.

"We walk around this snake and give it as much space as it wants," I said as casually as possible.

We walked several blocks more in silence; her eyes were darting everywhere, on the lookout for the next menace. After a while she said, somewhat accusingly, I thought, "Didn't you say there were no snakes in the city?" I had been expecting this, but all of my clever answers fled.

"There didn't used to be," I said, in my whiny ten-year-old voice.

The A-Mazing Central Market

I have always loved mazes. I used to pencil through the ones on the comic page of the Sunday paper and would even invent them myself. I was determined to go through a maze when I visited England (but didn't). If you wonder, as I did, if the word amaze is derived from maze, it is. The original meaning of amazed was "bewildered."

Now, when I feel an urge to experience a maze, I visit the Mercado Central. The market is a covered city block between Avenida Central and Avenida 1. It is a maze of narrow alleys with many turns, lined with kiosks overflowing with goods.

You can probably find anything you want in the Central Market. All of the expected things, of course, like meats, chicken, fish, produce and dozens of *sodas* (not soft drinks, but tiny restaurants) featuring cheap food. You can find turtle eggs, sewing thread and yarn, spices and herbs (medicinal and otherwise), handbags and back packs, luggage, paper plates, leather goods and real flowers, dishes and kitchen utensils, Christmas ornaments and Swiss Army knives, shoes, and now, even a beauty shop.

How to find them is another matter. So far I have found no signs to tell you where you are. But then, if the city doesn't label its streets, why bother with its alleys, all safely within the confines of a building?

I needed some black pepper in *granos* and some vanilla beans. I also bought some *bomba*. I learned of this from my friend Lillian, after I commented on how tasty the sauce on the chicken was at a luncheon. Lillian hates it. She says her maid says it is used to cover the taste of bad meat. According to Lillian, it is also used to bolster the flavor of tamales when the broth is weak. It's a mixture of fifteen ingredients, including garlic, cumin, onion, cilantro, bay leaf, thyme, oregano, different peppers and bouillon. It usually is layered in a plastic bag and looks like different colored sand. Quite pretty. If I don't like it, I'll just display it.

I play a game with myself in the mercado. (My status as an adult is sometimes tenuous.) I spot something I want in a particular kiosk, then wander off and away, then, after I am completely lost, try to find the kiosk again. This time it was a small bottle of mint flavoring. Eventually I did find it. I also went in search of the beauty shop Darrylle had told me about. His haircut looked good to me and it cost only ¢1,000. It took longer to find the beauty shop, which looks clean and new (which it is, being less than two months old). Men's haircuts are ¢1,000, women's ¢1,200 ($3.50). I stopped getting my hair cut professionally several years ago, after yet another beautician sheared me. I decided I could do as bad a job, for free. And I have.

But if you go there looking for the beauty shop, enter the market from Avenida 1 between the two fish markets facing the street. Be careful going up the two stairs that greet you. They look as if they have been eaten away by large rats. I didn't notice that when I was leaving and turned my ankle, and went flying flat, for the third time in six months. I don't think I have become clumsier; the walkways and sidewalks *are* treacherous. I've decided to look on the positive side of these little exercises. I call them my sidewalk greetings. Each time, I seem to land full force on one hand to catch my fall. The other hand is fiercely clutching my handbag. I am always picked up by at least six hands that put me back on my feet whether I want to be there or not. I actually would prefer to lie there a moment and collect my thoughts, but I seem to be an embarrassment to everyone, because there I am upright, like the rest of the world, although a bit dazed. Dazed in a maze, in this case.

The positive side of this is I have now labeled my pitched falls my "bone density tests." If I haven't broken my wrist, I'm still in good shape. Still in good shape, but not ready for the street, I went back into the maze.

Bus-it Around Town

Although from time to time I complain about how far I have to walk to my bus stop, in most cases, at least in the city, a bus stop is just a few blocks away. The public transportation system in Costa Rica is something to be envied. You can get to the farthest reaches of the country by bus. (I wish I could include train travel in that statement.) And in case you haven't noticed, there are many new buses in the city, not the second-hand school buses that used to be so common, but new Mercedes and other makes. The pollution is far less now.

When I first came to Costa Rica, I was downtown after a soccer game—the streets filled with celebrants and me looking for a bus home. All I could find were buses marked Desamparados. I knew the word meant "abandoned," and I thought, "Wow! They even have a special sign for when bus drivers have decided to leave their buses and celebrate winning a soccer game!" Now, of course, I know that Desamparados is a suburb of San José. You usually can count on buses to run, no matter what.

Mostly I travel around town. One of the best ways to get from what I consider downtown San José (using the National Theater as a landmark), to the area of Sabana Park is by one of the Cementerio buses. They stop at three places along Avenida 2, the main one being alongside the *Caja*, the tall building housing the Social Security offices, on Avenida 2 and Calle 5. One bus marked Fischel goes on the north side of town along Avenidas 1 and 3 west, passing near the AutoMercado and the main post office. The other one goes south on the Paseo de los estudiantes, turns to go past the Clínica Biblica, and then goes west. You can ride either one without getting lost in the boondocks. Beware of the *Periferico*. It means "periphery." Only take a bus labeled that if you have a supply of food and water and wish to tour all the poorer little barrios around the city. There is a *Periferico* bus stop at the University of Costa Rica. I haven't searched for other stops.

If you wish to go east, most of the buses begin and end either in front of the old Cine Capri (now an evangelical church) on Avenida Central near 11th St. or in front of MasXMenos. These buses will take you to San Pedro, Curridabat and parts east.

Buses for Heredia and Alajuela (including the airport) have stops on Avenida 2 near the Church and Parque la Merced.

I decided to visit the Tourist Bureau underneath the Plaza de la Cultura to see if they had any useful maps of bus routes. The only one they had (and it was under glass) is the same one I once had, which was published in *La Nación* in 1999 when they changed the bus routes. The two women in charge were singularly uninterested in helping me – something unusual in Costa Rica – but there were a lot of free brochures, including some with information about buses to the most popular beaches and tourist sites in the country.

The Museo de Oro is also there, so it was a good chance for me finally to visit. Admission is free for residents over 65; those under 65 pay ¢1000, and tourists pay ¢2800. It is well worth it. If you go there first, you will understand where the people who sell their trinkets and jewelry got the ideas for their designs. The ones in the museum are stunning. There are animals, humans, and objects. Some of the tiny figures are dressed in the regalia of the *caciques*, or chiefs, or maybe priests of that pre-

Columbian era. In their costumes they reminded me of the tiny man I met in Sao Salvador, Brazil. He was a holy man in some religion unfamiliar to me. He was a mild unprepossessing little man. He took us down into the cellar of his home to show us the altar where he held his services, then he gave me a picture of himself in the costume he donned for the occasion. Dressed in regalia of mask and feathers, with his body decorated, he seemed to have grown two feet, imposing enough to inspire awe. He could have been the model for one of the tiny figurines in the Museo de Oro.

The museum also has a wonderful collection of ceramic stamps, both flat and cylindrical, with designs to decorate material or bodies. Much nicer than tattooing. There are other displays depicting life in Pre-Columbian times.

Back again in the present, I walked to my bus stop near the *Caja,* wondering what other helpful information I could pass along. I would like to advise that if you don't know where the bus goes, just ask the driver, *"Usted pasa por_____"* and fill in where you want to go. That always worked for me until the day I asked the driver, *"Usted pasa por Munoz y Nanne?"* The driver nodded yes so I got on. And sure enough, we passed Munoz y Nanne—sailed right on past it at 30 miles an hour.

Sidewalk Cafés

Among the criteria I had for the place where I would retire were two that I would not call essential, but highly desirable. I wanted a place where bougainvillea grew and where city sidewalk cafés were as plentiful as the bougainvillea.

I fell in love with bougainvillea in Majorca, Spain, the first time I lived abroad, and that was where I also spent many happy hours in sidewalk cafés scribbling away in my lined notebooks. Bougainvillea abounds in Costa Rica but, unfortunately, sidewalk cafés are very rare in the city. I certainly can understand why – the rainy season and the wind.

Not long ago I toured the city looking for sidewalk cafés. I noticed that a few more places are putting tables outside their doors, especially on Avenida Central, which is such a pleasant place to walk and shop now that it is a pedestrian mall – or as the Ticos call it, the *bulevar.* Manolo's was the first to put out tables, and I understand that the owners went through some municipal red tape to get permission. The few tables are usually full. Recently I saw workmen on the avenida building two gazebos. With high hopes, I asked them if they were, by any chance, going to be cafés or perhaps kiosks for musicians. No, I was told, they would house ATM machines for the nearby bank. Sigh.

Recently the Hotel Bulevar, also on Avenida Central, put tables on its second floor balcony reminiscent of New Orleans. I had lunch up there the other day just to get the feel of it. It was an interesting experience looking down on the passing parade. I realized that sitting above the street was very much like being on safari. Looking down, I saw people in groups (herds?) or as solitary animals hurrying to and from their watering holes. I looked down upon obvious family groups, the young ones sticking close to the mothers, and the fathers looking protective.

I saw groups of people dressed the same, rare among humans but common among other animals. Here in Costa Rica the employees of many businesses and students of almost all schools wear uniforms. I watched the rushers and the amblers, the tall and the short, young lovers nuzzling each other, old lovers clinging to each other, and a few old-young couples – often old gringos with young

Ticas not an uncommon sight here, but more often found in the restaurants, bars and casinos. From my vantage point, I could watch the interaction between a young street beggar with twisted legs and the people passing by him. A lot of people in San José give to the less fortunate.

For a complete contrast, I visited the Cyber Cafe in the Las Arcadas building on Avenida 2. This café is below the street and provides an entirely different view. Of course, the traffic fumes are more noticeable, but we city dwellers learn to accept the noises and smells of the city just as our country friends put up with the sounds and smells of the country. In this café I had a view of moving legs and loads: backpacks and purses, grocery bags and briefcases. Very few faces were visible. I got caught up in the different gaits, which was fun, but not very restful. Too many people were rushing (or at least their legs were).

My last sit-down was in the oldest and largest outdoor café in San José: the Café París in the Gran Hotel de Costa Rica in the plaza in front of the National Theater. There I was on the same level as the people passing by. Perhaps it is sharing the same sidewalk and the possibility of making eye contact, but I felt more connected to others, and I liked that feeling.

Most of the people passing by were dressed in T-shirts and jeans, or in other very casual clothes. But every now and then a well-dressed person would come along. Seeing them made me remember the sidewalk cafés of Paris in the fifties. Sidewalk cafés define the City of Light. Even in winter the sidewalk cafés are operating with heaters outside to keep you comfortable. In San Francisco, even in the fog you can sit in an outdoor café. New York may put a railing around them, but they exist. Noisy Athens and all Greek islands have them. The largest sidewalk café I ever saw was in Oslo, Norway, a lovely city where the sidewalks are sometimes wider than the streets.

If Oslo can figure out a way to have them, surely the city planners who are doing such a good job with pedestrian malls can figure out how to put sidewalk cafés in San José.

Taxis – A Luxury Elsewhere, A Bargain Here

I take taxis quite often. My fare is seldom more than ¢450 (about $1.10), so when I find myself waving futilely as taxi after empty taxi drives past me, I have to struggle not to think they are purposely ignoring me because they know me and decide I am not worth their effort. But that seldom happens and I rarely wait more than five minutes to hail a cab successfully. I used to raise my arm high like I did in New York City until a Tico informed me that here you hold your arm no higher than three o'clock. I don't think a raised arm is considered rude; I think they can see you better or can be sure you are not just waving to a friend.

Many people sit in the front seat with the driver. I usually sit in the back, mainly because I don't like to struggle with a seat belt. Sitting in the back seat does cut down on conversation, but sometimes the radio does that. Occasionally I will ask a driver to turn down the volume. But my biggest struggle is to resist telling him how to best get to where we are going. I feel like Holly Hunter in the movie where she gives every cab driver in Washington, D.C., directions on the best route to take and why. Many times, I think the *taxistas* here unthinkingly take the same route no matter the time of day or the traffic. It is seldom useful to give a taxi driver an address based on the name of the street or avenue. Here we still use landmarks (try 200 meters south of the old *higuerón* tree, which was cut down years ago!). I do get annoyed when the *taxista* doesn't even know where the landmark is.

There are *pirata* taxis (pirates). These are cars without permits to which drivers have attached a taxi sign; and some even have a *maría* (the meter that tells you the price), but I avoid them. Although rare, most of the taxi crimes against passengers occur in pirate cabs. Licensed taxis have a yellow triangle on the front doors, usually with the number of the cab. Pirate cabs don't.

Once in a while a taxi driver will start asking me questions about how long I have lived here, am I married, etc. More often the two of us are preoccupied with our own thoughts. There are some rude drivers – if I had to drive in this traffic I think I would be a bit short at times – but most often drivers are pleasant and kind. The other day, I was in a taxi on Avenida 8, stalled in traffic, and it was an unusually hot day with the sun blazing. My driver pointed out a woman on the corner with a small baby trying to get a cab, and he asked if it was all right if he offered her a ride. I said, of course. She was very appreciative and he told her it was my kindness that was responsible. I hadn't even noticed her.

Other times, when I have two heavy bags of groceries or luggage, I have asked, with the offer of a tip, for help to my third floor apartment. I have never been refused. When I first came here I was told that it is not the custom to tip taxis. Usually I don't, but if I have called a cab from the house or if the driver does not start the *maría* until after I get in the taxi, I do tip. They are supposed to do this but the *maría* usually is already going and I must assume it was turned on just a second before I entered. If the driver says his *maría* is broken, I always ask, *"Cuánto va a costarme?"* (How much is it going to cost me?) before we go anywhere. When I arrived in Costa Rica the base price for a taxi was something like ¢80. Today taxis start at ¢340 but, with the exchange rate adjusting daily, the cost remains about the same for people with a dollar income. All in all, taxis are one of the best bargains in the city.

Taxista Advice

I had a chatty taxi driver the other day. I couldn't believe my luck when he stopped his taxi at the light on Avenida 2 next to the National Theater in a downpour. I had been standing in the rain for too long and losing hope by the minute. I was grateful he stopped, and I told him so.

By the time we were halfway home he knew I was here alone, had two children in the States and wrote a column about Costa Rica for *a.m.costarica.com*. When he asked what I wrote about, I told him, about the city, the parks, the *ferias*, the kindness of the Costa Rican people. After a bit he said, "Yes, but you must write about the bad things, too, or tourists will come here expecting only good things and get into trouble and never want to come back."

So, *Señor Taxista* (one of the many kind Costa Ricans I have met), here are some of the bad things — well, maybe. Tourists want the nitty-gritty about the beaches and the rain and cloud forests (in case you wondered, a cloud forest is just a rain forest with an altitude), and hotels and activities outside the city. My friends are right when they say I am a "city girl"; I would be as happy spending time in the seven greatest cities in the world as I would be gazing at the seven wonders of the natural world . . . well, nearly. It took my friend Sandy to inform me that cloud forests get their moisture from the clouds, not from rainfall. The trees trap the moisture from the low-hanging clouds. The bad news here is that, as the trees in the lowlands are cut, temperatures rise and so does the warm air, which pushes the clouds higher – out of reach of the trees in the cloud forest.

Another unfortunate thing to happen was President José Maria Figueres' announcement upon becoming president in 1994, that, if rich tourists could afford to spend $700 to come to Costa Rica, they could afford to pay $15 to see its wonderful national parks – cloud or otherwise. Granted, the fees to enter the national parks have been ridiculously low, but $15 per person? I winced when I heard this because I knew what would happen. Every small hotel-owner, every pension and bed-and-breakfast owner – everybody in the tourist business immediately had the same thought: "If they can pay $15 to see a park, they can pay more than the $20 (or whatever nice low price) they are paying for what I have."

And prices went up all over Costa Rica, without a concomitant rise in the quality of service, accommodations or product. Suddenly, Costa Rica was no longer the reasonably priced destination of natural wonders and gracious people.

The only thing that went down was the number of tourists who came to visit. It took a few years and a change in policy to recover from that, but prices, I think, are still too high. (Although with the world situation the way it is now, and hearing that the government is suggesting that hotels lower their prices, I suggest you negotiate.)

Another unfortunate (unfortunate is too tame a word – tragic is better) turn of events is the increase in the number of homeless children on the streets. This, too, involves government action, or lack of it. With the withdrawal of money for the Salvation Army shelters, some 200 children were simply dumped onto the streets.

If you walk in San José early in the morning, you will see the youngsters not in groups, but in lonely, and probably hungry, isolation, huddled in doorways or under sheets of cardboard near trash, waking up from a nightmare night. It is scary when a country gives up on its children.

Apropos of children's shelters: I thought the manager of the refuge made one very regrettable response to a government representative's remark that it was smelly and not very clean. He said that they didn't want to make the accommodation "so nice that kids don't care about improving their situation." (*The Tico Times*, July 6, 2001).

Most of these kids have moved from abusive, unloving (and probably dirt-poor) homes to the streets and then the shelter. What is there in their lives as a model to inspire a move to, say a one-bedroom apartment with a Jacuzzi? You should give them the best you can so they learn to be comfortable in nice surroundings and want to take care of them, and dream of making them even better. This is not to criticize what the manager was doing. I applaud that. I am sure he regrets that statement, or it may have been misinterpreted.

Well, I have come this far and I haven't really responded to the advice of my kind *taxista*. I would have liked to ask him to give me some ideas, but by then we had arrived home and he had a living to make in the rain and I wanted to dry off in my apartment. Maybe next time.

Street Smart

I am not. But having been pick-pocketed three times, having had a necklace ripped from my neck and having heard the stories of other people's misfortunes on the streets of San José, I have learned a few things.

First of all, I advise everyone to do what I did not do: report it to the police. Like most other people, I figured it would be useless because the police couldn't or wouldn't do anything, and it would just take a lot of futile time and paperwork. This is a perfect example of self-fulfilling prophecy: if no one reports the crime, the police will think there is little going on and do nothing.

33

However, according to the theory of critical mass, with all of us reporting our complaints, the police might decide that it would be more interesting to go after the perps than to process more paperwork.

And now some cautionary advice:

Women should clutch their purses firmly and, if it is a shoulder bag, hang it across their chests. Men, never carry your wallets in your back pockets. Beware of someone in front of you who "accidentally" drops his backpack or whatever he is carrying. Immediately clutch your handbag or wallet. His cohort is ready to rob you in the ensuing confusion. Men, beware of an attractive woman who seems to want your attention. While the two of you are smiling at each other and otherwise occupied, her partner in crime is going for your wallet. And you all probably know about the spot on your jacket ploy. If someone "accidentally" spills something on you, or you find your clothing suddenly covered with a gooey substance, before some friendly onlookers can help you wipe it off, run. Don't let them get near you. For women, if you are in a crowded bus and a young man becomes charmingly chummy and chats with you, make sure your purse is zipped up and as far from him as possible. He is after what is in it. And he is very clever at removing that wallet without your knowing it.

Being alert to these con people begins at the airport. A recent scam is for someone, seemingly a fellow passenger waiting in line with you, to pick up a passport and say, "Is this yours?" While you are distracted and searching your person to make sure you have your passport, his or her partner in crime is making tracks with your luggage. If you rent a car, you may discover after a few miles that you have a flat tire. Do not stop to check it. Drive as far as you can, even on the rim, to where it is safe. Someone who has been following you is waiting, perhaps under the pretense of offering help, to relieve you of everything you have brought with you.

I would love to witness the modern-day version of Fagin's School for Pickpockets. They are getting better and better at it. And they keep coming up with new and clever ways to take your possessions. They are often well dressed, well spoken and charming. Not so with muggers. According to Carolyn, who is pretty streetwise, muggers are, in fact, very stupid. So, she says, what you should do is ask them a question and while they are figuring out the answer, you run. If they have a weapon, she says you should throw your wallet as far as you can and while they are going after it, you run. Just don't run in the same direction as the wallet. I heard of someone in Santa Ana, who not only was mugged, but stabbed. He threw his wallet and, while they chased it, he got away. It seems that Carolyn is right; so I have bought another wallet to carry for throwing, but so far, the only question I can think of is,

"Excuse me, but when do you get off work?"

The Times, They are A-changing

Shortly after I first came to Costa Rica, I was downtown on Avenida 2 right after a football game that Costa Rica had won. I was trying to find my bus stop. People were celebrating in the street, yelling, drinking beer, and congratulating each other. Cars could not move; people could barely move. I looked around. Not a policeman in sight. I wanted order, although I had to admit no one was acting in a threatening manner and nothing was getting out of hand.

"Where," I shouted at someone, "are the police?"

He shrugged. "The police have to celebrate, too," he said.

This was before the police had uniforms, so who could tell? Costa Rica had no army and didn't want its policemen to get any ideas by giving them guns and letting them wear uniforms. I've never forgotten the positive energy I felt, the lack of hostility, even in a big crowd.

Usually a walk downtown cheers me up. Especially when I am blue, the combination of the exercise and the benign bustle of people lift my spirits. But the other day, for the first time, being downtown depressed me. I had been feeling fine before I walked onto Avenida Central. First I encountered six brown-garbed police persons standing in a circle talking to each other. I thought, no, no, you should be looking out for the pedestrians. I walked farther along the Avenue and beheld dozens of police in spanking new blue uniforms and, beyond them, row after row of blue motorcycles, also spanking new. They filled two blocks of the pedestrian walk that is Avenida Central.

I asked one of the uniformed finest what was this all about. (I have always found the police here most willing to inform lowly civilians about what is going on. When the Nicaraguan Embassy was taken hostage some years ago, the police standing outside the yellow tape were most forthcoming in keeping me up to date as I stopped on my way downtown).

Now I was informed that the police department had just received 200 new motorcycles. My heart sank. Are there enough police to ride all those motorcycles, I asked? Oh yes, he allowed. But they are all on foot now. My heart sank further. No more walking patrols. Even if they often seemed to be talking to each other, they were there and visible, and I felt safer with them around. I counted five new buses. Big buses complete with metal mesh windows. But we have so much traffic now, I said, how will these buses and motorcycles fit in the streets? He smiled reassuringly. That's why we also have some Vespas and smaller motor bikes, he said. Arggh!

Every one of the newly uniformed police also had a shiny new helmet. I want them to be safe, but how can they see much with those helmets and visors? And if they see anything, like a street mugger, can they just dump their motorcycle and give chase on foot?

I tried to look pleased. There was even a clown twisting balloons in various shapes to help celebrate. I was becoming depressed. Then, following some signal that I missed, the blue garbed police mounted their shiny blue motorcycles and revved them, ready to go.

In a few moments our lovely car-free *bulevar* was filled with blue smoke and a bad smell. Pedestrians, including myself, covered faces, some with the necks of their tee shirts, others with their hands. Would these motorcycles, I wondered, be allowed to go up and down this mall on a regular basis?

The one thing I did not ask the other day was, who had paid for all these new buses and motorcycles and uniforms?

The Magic of City Parks

It's been a long time since I have walked in downtown San José in the early morning. I had been visiting INS – the National Insurance Building – for a couple of days going through the red tape necessary for a claim on my health insurance. At ten minutes to eight the traffic was still light, the air was still fresh, and the streets had few cars. Mainly there were pedestrians rushing to their jobs in offices, agencies and stores that had yet to open.

The day before, on my third visit, I had forgotten my ID, so I was unable to collect my money. (All bureaucratic endeavors seem to require three visits.) There had been a line of over fifty people at 2 p.m., which made me think that Ticos must like to do business in the afternoon and perhaps if I returned the next morning as soon as INS opened, I could complete my business sooner. I was right. So there I was, back on the street with nearly three hours until my next appointment.

I decided to walk through two of my favorite parks, Parque de España and the Parque Nacional, which I noticed had been unveiled, or I should say, unfenced, since it has been surrounded by a blue metal fence for months.

The Parque de España is a mini rain forest in the middle of the city, right across from the INS Building. The park is small – about half a city block and between two streets that are on different levels. Ivy-covered trees tower above and shade the brick walkways in the park. There is even a bamboo grove. The well-tended beds of flowers – ginger and bird of paradise – add color to the enveloping greenery. It is cool and shadowed there. There are concrete benches where you can sit and feel as if you are far from the city (and still within walking distance of home). On the upper level of the park stands an exuberant fountain and a huge statue of a conquistador with a sword nearly as tall as he.

After spending a while in the Parque de España, I visited the park across the street from the school known as the *edificio metálico*. I still don't know the name of the park, which is right next to Parque Morazán. Perhaps it is named after Daniel Oduber Quiros, President of Costa Rica in the 1970's, because there is a statue of him at the edge of the park, with three plaques of his quotes. One says, "*El verdadero fin de nuestros esfuerzos no es la riqueza sino el hombre.*" ("The true goal of our efforts is not riches, but mankind.") Another, "*Los parques nacionales – a los que mi gobierno ha dado prioridad – serán santuarios de la vida de ayer y de la mañana.*" ("The national parks – a priority of my government – will be sanctuaries of the life of yesterday and tomorrow.") Visit the park and check out the third quote for yourself.

The Parque Nacional, which is across the street from the new government building, has been in the process of restoration for so long that I hardly remember what it was like. It doesn't matter. Today the park seems much sunnier, as if some trees have been removed. The trees that remain seem to have individual personalities. Some are regal.

The walkways have been enlarged considerably and the space around the central sculpture is much larger, ready to accommodate government officials and their audiences. The gazebo overlooking the pond is a lovely spot to sit (although I would have put a roof on it so park visitors would have a haven during a sudden *aguacero*).

Besides a number of lovely flowerbeds, the restoration has included more benches and picnic tables with little toadstool seats, and hurray! the park is dotted with elegant, nicely designed, trash containers. I didn't see an empty bottle or a piece of paper anywhere. We're learning. Just give us enough proper places to throw our trash and we'll throw it there. The park is a lovely place to take your lunch in the middle of a busy day, and now it merits its name.

The Parque de España, however, is my favorite because of the memory I have of my son's visit. We stopped there one afternoon to rest and, sitting side by side on one of the concrete benches in the quiet shade of the tall trees, we talked, and it was one of those magical times when we said what was in our hearts, not what was on our minds.

Sunday in the Park

Every time I go west from San José to Escazú or Pavas, I have to pass Sabana Park and think that I would like to spend some time there. Sabana Park is San José's biggest municipal park and similar to New York's Central Park, although not as large. It contains a lake with a fountain and an island, soccer and baseball fields, pony and horseback rides, picnic tables, two stadiums and a museum, paths galore to walk along and roads winding through it, a sculpture garden and trees, trees and more trees. From my bus I see hundreds of people enjoying this green space in the city. San José has many parks, but most of them are just one square block. This park is the size of an airport landing field.

The uniqueness of Sabana Park is that it once was the first International Airport of Costa Rica. By 1955, air traffic had increased so much that a larger airport was built near Alajuela (where it is today). Light air traffic and private aircraft continued to use the Sabana location until the early seventies, when even that was moved either to Alajuela or to a city airport in Pavas.

The former air terminal in Sabana, designed by architect José Maria Barrantes, was a fusion of Spanish Colonial with more modern purity of line. It was remodeled by architects Jorge Bertheau and Edgar Brenes into what is now the very gracious Museo de Arte Costarricense. Today the park and the museum truly belong to the people. Entry to the park is free, and on Sundays to the museum.

When two new friends, Alexis and James, invited me to join them for a picnic in the park on Sunday, I happily accepted. James was able to park the car on the road next to the museum, and from there we walked looking for an empty table. Just as we thought there was no such thing, one appeared. We were suspicious that there must be something wrong with the location. But although soccer players and rolling soccer balls surrounded us, it was lovely. Alexis laid a tablecloth on the round cement table, put cushions on the benches (how luxurious can you get?) and began to unload salad after salad from their cooler. All in all, there were five salads, each a gastronomical delight from a different country. All delicious.

With a small wedge of cheese – my contribution from the last of some Stilton I had brought from the States – we had a very French picnic. We were, James noted, the only table sporting a bottle of wine. Children were everywhere, as were the soccer balls. One tiny toddler, just new to walking, was still able to coordinate his little bowed legs to give a solid kick to a moving soccer ball. I always marvel at how young they start here. In the States, they learn to wield a bat.

After our lunch, we walked over to the Museum to enjoy the wide range of art on display. I had expected more people because of the free entrance, but there were very few and we could wander and look and talk without fear of bumping into or annoying anyone.

As we drove through the park on our way out, Alexis pointed out all the recently planted eucalyptus trees, along with the newly built children's recreational area. When the park was first created, the lake that had been drained for the airport was restored. It appears to be fed by a spring. Hundreds of trees, now grown tall, were planted.

I realized that while we were there, we had seen lots of people, plenty of food and drink, even animals, but I don't recall shooing one fly, swatting one mosquito, or seeing one ant (or sand flea) during our lunch. Could that be possible? Just to make sure, we went back for another picnic a couple of weeks later. We did shoo away a couple of flies and had to say no to a couple of food-seekers, but the only other addition was a tiger and a lion – the kind that walk on two feet – that were having their pictures taken with the children. On our next visit, we plan to get a table right next to the lake.

Butterflies in the City

The other day I was on the bus going from the Plaza del Sol into the center of town when a butterfly flew into the bus and made a gentle landing on my blouse near my waist. It was a beautiful butterfly, mainly brown with scarlet spots. I watched it for some time, trying not to disturb it, as it batted its wings and rested. It reminded me of the days some years ago, when, new to Costa Rica, I would walk downtown on Tenth Avenue and feel as if I was literally surrounded by butterflies. San José is no Paris, but I don't remember ever seeing butterflies above the streets of Paris. It was another reason for me to love Costa Rica.

The butterfly had enough of my shirt and took off for the passenger behind me and settled on his shirt. The passenger welcomed his visitor, as I had done, until he, too, was abandoned and the butterfly flew to the front of the bus. This time it settled on the head of the bus driver. I could see it in the driver's rear view mirror. There was something utterly charming about a butterfly perched on the curly black hairline of the bus driver. I was even more charmed because I thought the driver must know the butterfly was there (after all, if I could see it in the mirror, so could he), and yet he did nothing to disturb it.

I watched, fascinated, for several minutes, full of kind thoughts about a world where butterflies were free, and I remembered some weeks before when I had attended the 50th anniversary celebration of the abolition of the Costa Rican army in the Plaza de la Democracia. I was sitting about fifty feet away from where the President of the country, two former Presidents, and a number of other dignitaries were standing. I was hardly aware of any secret service types. Now on the bus, I smiled as I thought about that wonderful moment at the end of the speeches when, instead of a twenty-one gun salute or a display of fighter planes overhead, the Presidents and dignitaries, along with about sixty school children, opened the white boxes they were holding and released hundreds of butterflies. And now, here was this bus driver, a product of fifty years of peace, allowing a butterfly to perch on his head – perhaps it was one of those that had been released that day.

The butterfly shifted its position and flapped its crimson dotted wings against the driver's forehead. Instinctively, up came the driver's hand to swat the spot. Then the driver vigorously brushed his hair to rid himself of the nuisance. The butterfly disappeared. I leaned out of my seat, wanting so to see it, still intact, shrugging to right itself, and perhaps flitting off to another temporary rest. But it did not appear. It could well be lying crumpled and wounded on the floor of the bus, next to the gas pedal. I wanted to rush up and rescue it, or at least shout, "It was only a butterfly!" But I was too self-conscious and afraid I might appear deranged. I sighed. Even in Costa Rica, things change, and things are not always the way you think they are.

It was only much later that I realized that other passengers must have seen what I saw (at least those who could look in the mirror), and they would have understood had I gone up to the front of the bus to rescue the butterfly. Butterflies have to be saved so that each year they can help celebrate another year without a military.

Getting Comfortable in a New Culture

A Christmas Carol to Costa Rica

The quality of life is not measured simply by efficiency (as the Italians learned during the time of Mussolini) nor by material things. For all of those people who have asked me why I moved to Costa Rica and do I still like it, here is my response – and my Christmas Carol to Costa Rica, which includes twelve reasons for living here. I am borrowing from some things I wrote after just three years in the country. Costa Rica, like other countries in the world, has changed, but even after ten years, these reasons still hold.

I was originally drawn to this country because it has no army and, as a result, it has developed a peace mentality. Costa Ricans do not like confrontations and are not greatly into competition. Because I am competitive in games but not happy about competition in life, I felt comfortable here.

I was charmed (and still am) when Ticos thank me. They don't just say *"Gracias,"* they usually say, *"Gracias, muy amable."* Which means, "Thank you, you're very kind." Being told I am kind often enough makes me *see* myself as kind and wanting to be more so.

My life here is further enhanced each time a *Tico* says, "You're welcome." Here they don't say, as they do in most other Spanish-speaking countries, *"No hay de que"* or *"De nada"* ("For nothing"); they say, *"Con mucho gusto,"* or *"Con gusto."* ("With much pleasure" or, more loosely, "The pleasure is mine.") My friend Jerry has said more than once that giving and receiving are the same thing and Ticos seem to believe this. I have been trying to remember to say both *"Gracias, muy amable"* and *"Con mucho gusto."* Language is a powerful influence on attitude.

I enjoy walking in downtown San José, in spite of the traffic and challenging sidewalks. When I first came

47

here and mixed with the people on the streets, I thought, "There are as many pedestrians here as there are in New York City at Christmas time – but without the stressful energy or hostility." Instead I find myself energized and uplifted. I also noticed that most Costa Ricans have fine postures. Almost to a person, they walk tall and proud. It is a pleasure to see them, and seeing them reminds me to straighten up. It is surprising how much better you feel when you walk tall.

I have had a number of occasions to experience the health care of Costa Rica, both private and public (there is national health coverage here). The cost of medical care is much less than in the United States, and I always have felt more cared for and cared about in my experiences here. Even in the overworked and under-supplied national hospitals, I have found attention and compassion. It outweighs the lack of Kleenexes. The last time I was in the Hospital Calderón Guardia emergency section, they passed out lunches at noon and coffee and snacks in the late afternoon to the waiting patients.

Although business transactions are not always speedy, how can you not like a country where it is the law that every public building must have a public bathroom? (That doesn't mean they must supply paper.) And it is true one spends considerable time waiting in lines. This is where I get a lot of my reading done. I've waited in lines in many countries, and I'll take an orderly, friendly queue of Ticos any day.

There is a custom here that many North Americans have picked up, that of brushing cheeks when seeing a friend or acquaintance. In the States, after an initial handshake following an introduction, I seldom touch that person again, certainly not my travel agent, my doctor or my landlord. Here, I do. Touching cheeks makes me feel a connectedness to others – and when you think about it, is much more sanitary than a handshake.

On the comfort front, it is hard to beat the climate in the Central Valley of Costa Rica. I have lived where there were fifteen-foot snowdrifts and where I became accustomed to perspiration dripping down my neck all the time. Living where I need neither air conditioning nor a heater is such a pleasure, and I'm sure, far healthier.

Because the climate makes for multiple growing seasons, fresh vegetables and fruits are available most of the year. If one were a vegetarian, one could live very cheaply here.

And finally, what clinched my love affair with Costa Rica was discovering that their national bird is the *Yigüirro*. The *Yigüirro* (which I can't even pronounce) is very similar to the U.S. robin but smaller, and much less colorful. The *Yigüirro* neither threatens anyone's existence (it certainly is not a bird of prey), nor is it a rare or endangered species. It is a common little dun-colored bird – an "Everybird," if you will. I think a country that chooses the *Yigüirro* as its national bird has something to say to the rest of the world about peaceful co-existence, humaneness, self esteem and equality.

Culture Shock Happens

More and more people seem to be considering moving to Costa Rica. Some because they will retire soon and see Costa Rica as an easy and reasonable place to live. Some have fallen in love with the country on a visit. Others are just unhappy where they are and want a place where war and consumerism are not top priorities and fear is not pandemic. Whether or not to move to Costa Rica is entirely an individual decision. As for what to expect, I can only relate *my* experience.

Any move to a new culture is not easy. I learned early that referring to the way things were done at home (even mentally) was not helpful, and that the sooner I stopped translating colones into dollars when pricing things, the better. After a short time, I found the question, "How much is that in *real* money?" from other (usually visiting) North Americans from the States, not even slightly funny.

The Costa Rican name for people from the U.S. is *estadounidenses*. That is a mouthful, but Costa Ricans consider themselves Americans, too, in the sense that their country is part of Central America, and they tend to resent the statement, "I am an American."

Upon my arrival, I enrolled in a school to improve my Spanish and was enchanted with the lovely view of the surrounding mountains from my bus stop. The people there were friendly and helpful and complimented me on my Spanish. The wife of my host family was a great cook. I had few responsibilities.

After I left school and the home of my host family, I moved into an apartment in Sabanilla, which I soon found was too chilly for me, so I moved to Barrio Dent. After living in Costa Rica just six months, I began to wonder if I had made the right choice. This thought came after living for a month in a three-bedroom furnished apartment for which I was paying $653 and had signed a year's lease. The apartment was without charm. The kitchen was badly lighted, my TV got 1½ stations, the washing machine didn't work properly and the living room rug was filthy. I was involved in an ongoing disagreement with my landlord over what came first – my second $653 deposit (he wanted an outrageous two months' deposit), or doing something about my complaints.

Each time I left the apartment I felt as if I had a bushel-basket over my head whenever I tried to accomplish the simplest of errands. I was beginning to find Spanish an ugly language and no longer wanted to study it. What good would it do anyway – the people spoke so rapidly or in such strange dialects I would never understand them? I was tired of bland rice and beans. To add to all of this, I knew that more than once I had broken a cardinal rule of Costa Rica: I lost my temper. I am sure I broke other unwritten rules that I didn't even know about.

I didn't want to go back to the States, but I didn't want to be where I was either. I was suffering from "expatriate malaise"– or culture shock. Vaguely I understood this, and that I needed cheering up (and some spicy food), so I took myself downtown to the Tin Jo restaurant. I had read that they served organic vegetables and Szechuan dishes. I ordered a glass of Imperial beer, *bien fria* (still my favorite beer) and, having my notebook with me, started writing down all of my complaints. My beef with asparagus arrived; the organic asparagus was cooked to perfection. That was something positive, so I felt it only fair to also write down all the plusses of my present life.

Culture shock is an abstract concept. Generally expatriates, if they have chosen the country in which they are living, like the culture and the people – in the abstract. It is the everyday behavior and actions of the local people that they find frustrating and off-putting. By the same token, their own behavior is baffling and irritating to the people. And guess who has to adapt? Unless, of course, like many North Americans in countries like Saudi Arabia, you live in compounds isolated from the locals, their customs and their behavior.

On the plus side, I noted that the people were kind and friendly even though it was not easy to make close friends with Ticos unless one spoke fluent Spanish or married into a family. The weather was near perfect. I did more walking than I had ever done. Food was plentiful and cheap.

One of the best features of my apartment was its location. It was within walking distance of just about everywhere I wanted to go. The Centro Cultural Costarricense Norteamericano was just five minutes away. I spent hours there in the library reading English language newspapers and magazines, and I could check out books. The AutoMercado was just a few blocks farther. It was a large supermarket and it was always fun finding new items they were importing from other countries. The Cine Megaly was just twelve minutes away, and they showed the latest American movies with Spanish subtitles. All of these plusses were things that connected me to my home country, however, and were attachments I continued to need. I would never become a Costa Rican, I despaired. I would always be a gringa.

After lunch I walked around San José. Walking made me feel better. People returned my smile; I heard the gracious way Ticos say please and thank you. The energy of the city gave me energy.

I weathered the attack of the blues and within weeks found a roommate who was a better cook even than I and very compatible. My landlord came through with all of his promises and we agreed to put the rest of my deposit into a CD, where it would collect interest. I began to expand my circle of friends and activities.

Recently I have been feeling blue again. I think it started when I attended the peace rally. I wasn't carrying a sign and everyone knew I was a gringa. No one returned my smile.

"Your government says democracies don't start wars, but your country has started more wars in the past twenty years than any other country, and now it wants to start another one."

"I know. It doesn't make sense," was all I could say. Since then I have been aware that I am getting far fewer smiles in return to mine, and instead of the usual "*gracias, es muy amable*," or "*con mucho gusto*," there is silence. Perhaps I am just being paranoid, but today I pulled out the gray T-shirt that I bought on my visit in 1990. It has a big silver peace sign on it with the word for peace in twenty-nine languages. Maybe if I put this on I'll get a few smiles again and feel better.

Everyone should have Someone at Thanksgiving

Thanksgiving is my favorite holiday. I like it because it's one holiday that seems to have no axe to grind, except, of course, for the turkey. It's just about sharing food and being glad to be alive. I have had some wonderful Thanksgivings in my life, and the best ones included having at the table someone who otherwise would have been alone. Thanksgiving is a time to bring in orphans and share.

This year I'm very lucky, I'm having Thanksgiving with Jean and Rich. But my first Thanksgiving in Costa Rica was a pretty sad affair. I had not been here long, I felt I didn't know anyone well enough to invite to a Thanksgiving dinner, and I hadn't been invited to one. I was feeling pretty lonely and sorry for myself. So I did what I used to do as a child when my world was not going well – I went to bed, hoping that tomorrow would be better.

On that particular Thanksgiving, I was living in a small apartment in Sabanilla, and I crawled into bed as soon as it was dark. I actually went to sleep but was awakened around nine o'clock by the thumping of a drum and the strumming of a bass. Somewhere nearby someone was having a party or playing one very loud CD. Earplugs weren't working. Besides, I was hungry. I had gone to bed without supper. I really wanted a turkey dinner, but it was my own fault. I hadn't done anything to get one.

Sleep was out of the question. I remembered that casinos had recently opened in San José. Many years ago I worked as a keno runner in a Lake Tahoe casino. They are great places to go and just hang out. People are there, and a woman alone at night has no problems. I dressed and walked across the road to the bus stop, conveniently close. In no time I was going skyward in the elevator to the 17th floor of the Holiday Inn to the Aurola Casino, one of the first casinos to open in San José. I walked over to the roulette table and stood for a moment watching a lone young woman play.

"Come join me," she invited. "Maybe we can gang up on this croupier."

Soon we were chatting away and having a good time in spite of our losing. I've forgotten her name, so I will call her Priscilla. She was from Santa Barbara, California. After a short while, her companion came over from the rummy table. Priscilla introduced us. I shall call him Miles. We confessed that we were losing but having a good time. He said, "Well, I've just won nearly $400. Time to quit and have dinner." I began to say my goodbyes. Priscilla asked me if I had had dinner. No, I confessed, I had not.

"Please won't you join us for dinner, if we can get something like dinner at this hour?"

I said I would be delighted to, and the three of us went into the dining room, on the same floor as the casino. There on the menu was a complete Thanksgiving dinner, which they were still serving. Costa Rican restaurants had just begun to attempt North American-style Thanksgiving dinners, so it was not the best I have ever eaten, but it was one of the best Thanksgivings I remember.

A Funny Thing Happened on the Way to the Theater

This is a true story. At any rate, the charming young man named Say who told me this story said it was true. Actually, when I asked him if it was really true, he said, "I don't even know you, why would I lie to you?" Now that is a question with many interesting ramifications.

The story came about as we were both eating Angie Theologos' delicious *bocas* at the exhibition of her husband Jim's lively paintings. We were standing on the mezzanine of the Centro Cultural Costarricense Norteamericano in Los Yoses, a frequent venue of art exhibitions.

I was explaining to Say how to get to the Little Theatre in Bello Horizonte where the LTG (The Little Theatre Group of Costa Rica) was presenting Agatha Christie's *Ten Little Indians*.

"You know where *Los Anonos* Bridge is?" I asked. He nodded. "Well, you go over the bridge – the suicide bridge – on the old road to Escazú." Then I blushed and apologized for my insensitive use of the word suicide. Say is a Tico.

"That's all right," he assured me. "We call it that, too." Say, it turned out, is an emergency management technician — a rescue worker. We both agreed that there are times when you make jokes and laugh in order not to cry. He told me that one night his crew was called out on a report that someone had jumped from that bridge. When they arrived, they saw a man lying on the rock some sixty feet below — the "target rock" they call it, because that is where the unfortunate people usually land. Before heading down to the rock, they saw that the person was moving. He was still alive! They hurried down, and there was a man sitting up holding his wrist.

"My wrist hurts," he said.

The stunned crew examined him and had him stand up. He seemed to be perfectly fine except for a broken wrist.

"Did you go off the bridge?" one of them asked.

He said that he had, but that on his way down, a gust of wind came and lifted him up and he had floated the last six meters or so. "My wrist hurts," he complained again. He seemed unimpressed with his miraculous trip.

The crew helped him back up to the bridge, where an ambulance and the police were waiting. There the police informed him that, after his broken wrist had been attended to, he was under arrest. Attempting suicide is against the law in Costa Rica, as it is in some other countries. It would be interesting to attend his trial, I thought. With his luck, he would get off because there were no witnesses, and who would know if he jumped or was just testing some scientific phenomenon?

That was the story that Say told me. Now I wonder if perhaps it isn't just part of the folklore known as "urban legend." And maybe Say's asking me, "Why would I lie to you, I don't even know you?" is the Tico way of letting you know your leg is being pulled.

How to Think of Bus Drivers as Poets

I feel very lucky. So much of the rest of the world is sweltering in record-breaking heat, dodging tornados, or in danger of being swept away in a flash flood, and I wake up to mild, sunny days and blue skies that turn warm and then cool in the evenings (sometimes with rain in the afternoon). The climate in Costa Rica is still very livable. I wonder how long this will last.

In the distance, on the western horizon, there is a layer of smog. When I moved into this apartment about seven years ago, there was no smog. But seven years ago there weren't so many cars. I used to walk past little houses with garages or carports (every house has one or the other) that had been turned into an extra room or a patio. Now, these garages and carports have cars in them – sometimes two, although I can't figure out how they can fit two cars into some of these tiny spaces. It makes me wonder how much cars are contributing to the warming of the world and when will it be felt here? I know they are contributing to the air and noise pollution in Costa Rica.

In New York, a distraught resident who was threatened by a driver after he made some impolite comments about the driver's horn honking, decided to take a less aggressive way to relieve his tension. He began writing "honkus." A honku is based on the charming Japanese poem, the haiku, but the seventeen syllables are devoted to drivers who honk their horns. This disgruntled recipient of noise began pasting them around New York.

Sunday, I was riding the Sabana/Cementerio bus, which goes across town. I boarded at the bus stop next to the *Caja* building. There is little traffic in the city on Sundays, but I soon noticed that my driver had honked his horn twice in a matter of two blocks. He honked at each traffic light when the car in front had not jumped ahead as soon as the light changed. Instead of letting my annoyance get the best of me, I decided to make up a honku and meanwhile just count the times he honked his way to our destination. He honked at lights, at pedestrians who had to run for their lives and even at other buses just to wave at the drivers. The man seemed to have one hand permanently pushing his horn while he drove with the other.

We passengers looked at one another and rolled our eyes but, of course, said nothing. By the time we reached the Sabana, my driver had honked twelve times, and I was wondering if he was going to give me a baker's dozen. At this corner we hit a traffic jam because a street had been closed. In his frustration, he honked five more times, trying to get cars that had no power to do anything, to move. When I got off the bus I realized that my driver/poet had honked his own haiku, and thus saved me the trouble of coming up with one.

Costa Rican-Style Marketing on Streets and Buses

A couple of weeks ago I decided to accept every piece of paper offered to me on the street – these are advertisements handed out, often by very young people. Of course, once I decided to do that, the people handing out these notices seemed to disappear. But I do have a few. One announced a special at Quiznos for sandwiches for ¢695 (under $2). I can't find that one. But I had already been to Quiznos and was surprised when my bill was considerably less than usual. That piece of paper explained why.

Many of these ads are for schools. I have two of them. One says you can get your high school diploma (and with this announcement receive a 50% discount on enrollment). It lists the *ventajas* (advantages), including comfortable classrooms, excellent teachers, a *soda* (coffee shop), and individual attention. And classes are held day and night.

Another one offers free enrollment into a university where you can learn English and how to operate computers. It tells of the jobs that you will be prepared for.

Another small piece of paper I accepted advertises a Colombian beauty shop. It then lists the prices of all the various services. It would be interesting to compare these prices with those in other countries. A haircut for women is ¢2000, ($5.00), a pedicure ¢3000 ($7.50). The biggest price is for painless permanent makeup – probably eyeliner for

¢25,000 ($62.50). I was recently looking for eyeliners that don't run and they were over ¢3,000, so maybe over a lifetime, ¢25,000 is a bargain.

And finally we have an advertisement that begins with a testimonial from a satisfied customer of the *Caciques*. These "chiefs" helped her daughter overcome her drug addiction, and now she has a good job. The little flyer said that these *Caciques*, by means of prayer and secrets of the "Mother of the Jungle" and "Mother Nature," will cure whatever ails you, from impotence to drug addiction. They guarantee their work. How can one go wrong?

I certainly don't mind this method of advertising. I can always shake my head "no" if I don't want the piece of paper offered to me.

Then there are the people who are allowed to get on the city buses and sell their small items for usually ¢100 each (25 cents) to help some organization or other. Usually these people give their pitch for a couple of blocks, often in a stylized sing-song, then walk through the bus to collect money and hand out whatever they are selling and then get off. I have donated to various causes and once to a young man who told the sad story of his family. His little sister was sick, and his house was destroyed by a flood. If he could get up in front of a busload of people and tell his sad plight to us with such feeling, I felt he deserved help. But yesterday when I got on the bus some man was standing at his seat delivering a religious tirade that went on until we got to our final bus stop downtown.

He held some book in his hand (which seemed too small to be a Bible) and had a number of arm movements that he kept repeating. I was very annoyed at having my ride interfered with. I glanced around the bus to see others' reactions. Typical of Costa Ricans, most of them were pretending that he wasn't there. Typical North American that I am, I looked annoyed, feeling put upon as a captive audience. I am sure their blood pressures stayed normal while mine mounted.

My favorite street salesman is the "statue" that stands on a box near the Plaza de la Cultura. Dressed in a long white robe with a hood, and with a painted white face, he stands perfectly still until you put some money in the tin in front of him to help keep the environment intact and the world at peace. Then, like a mechanical doll, he bows and waves a thank you. Being in favor of both of the products he is selling, I usually put something in the tin and get my thanks.

Uniforms are the Mode Here

There is a preschool day-care facility on the corner, down the hill from my apartment. The other day on my way to catch the bus, I noticed that the children in the yard now have uniforms. Their uniforms are little gray T-shirts and matching shorts made of that soft cotton used in light sweats, the only decoration an emblem of the school. Boys and girls were dressed alike. My immediate thought was, how fortunate for the mothers, no ironing and easy care. For the children, no decisions or fighting about what they are going to wear.

I remember when President Clinton came out in favor of school uniforms in the U.S. While others decried the loss of freedom, I liked the idea. I have always liked the idea. President Clinton grew up in a family headed by a working mother just as I did. We were closer to poor than rich. I never thought much about that, but I do remember wishing I could go to a Catholic school because I heard they taught Greek and Latin – and because the kids wore uniforms. Uniforms are a great equalizer. In Costa Rica, uniforms are the law. Once all school children had to wear

60

the dark blue trousers (or skirts) and lighter blue shirts. Now only public schools must adhere to those colors, while private schools may choose different colors. Girls can wear trousers as well as skirts. In some schools different grades or levels wear different uniforms. Wearing uniforms is even the custom in some companies and banks here. Casino employees have "sort of" uniforms.

Some uniforms are quite attractive. The *Banco de Costa Rica* has a new uniform (new to this unobservant eye) that incorporates the colors of the flag, with the men wearing red ties and the women red scarves, white blouses and blue pants or skirts. Uniforms at work solve a lot of problems, too. No one can complain that you are not dressed appropriately. And making the decision in the morning about what to wear – especially for women – has to be so much simpler here. Cheaper, too. Of course, how you look in the uniform is a different matter. That might encourage people – both men and women – to get into shape because the same outfit can look so different on different people.

When I first moved here the police did not wear uniforms. In most countries, of course, they do. I was told that "the people" did not want them to get any ideas about their importance; besides, wearing uniforms would make them look too much like an army. Things have changed since then. Now the police have uniforms and cars labeled *policia*. But the Costa Rican attitude towards uniforms makes one realize how different cultures are

Meanwhile, back at the preschool, I stopped a minute to watch the children play. The little boys were doing their best to get their new uniforms as dirty as possible. One little boy actually jumped feet first on another. I expected a cry of pain and running to the teacher, but the only sound came from me as I empathized with the jumped-upon. He just rolled over to avoid the next onslaught. The little girls were pursuing more demure activities. I can watch little kids with the same fascination that other people watch birds or other animals. Many years ago, my husband and I were research assistants in the schools of Ipswich, Massachusetts. Our job was to observe school children at play, hoping to see if there was a correlation between the friends they chose, the ones they gravitated to, and their later achievement in whatever they set out to do. Part of this research had us standing in the schoolyard with our clipboards and writing down who played with whom. I enjoyed those days.

I tore myself away from these children and my memories and hurried to catch my bus, which, of course, passed the intersection just as I was twenty-five yards from it. As it passed, I thought how interesting it was that bus drivers here do not wear uniforms. In most other societies, that's one group that usually does.

Learning the Umbrella Ballet in San José

Here it is my eighth "green season" in Costa Rica and I still haven't become a member in good standing of the umbrella ballet in downtown San José. Everyone else seems to glide along, skillfully raising and lowering their umbrellas, tipping and bobbing and wielding them like Isadora Duncan managing her scarves. I, on the other hand, careen and stagger and bump with my muttered litany of *perdón, disculpe,* oops! *Lo siento.* I can't seem to get the right rhythm. My umbrella is just not part of me.

Sometimes I see someone especially skillful and follow that person and mimic her moves. This works pretty well but tends to take me where I don't want to go.

It's not that I'm a klutz. For years I had the habit of reading while I walked, even in the streets of San José. I started doing it when I was a kid when I never seemed to have enough time to read. I discovered I could use the half-mile walk to and from school for that purpose. And my habit was born. I've had few mishaps, even here, with all of the irregularities and potholes in the sidewalks. So for the first five years or so I continued to walk and read. There are few people who do this, but when I see someone walking along with his/her nose in a book, I feel a real affinity.

I finally quit because I realized that I must look quite mad, given the condition of the sidewalks – and it was dangerous. I also realized that things we learn to do as kids or are exposed to growing up come to us so much easier than the things we learn to do as adults, whether it is studying a language, driving a car, playing cards, being polite, or walking with an umbrella.

I grew up in a small town. The sidewalks were never full of people, except during a parade, and when it rained we usually stayed indoors. As a child, I never had to maneuver in a crowd with an umbrella, nor did I ever see a grownup doing it. I've had to learn it as an adult. Native *josefinos* are probably given umbrellas when they are three years old. There are lots of tiny umbrellas for sale in the *mercados*.

Umbrellas are tricky things. They can turn inside out, throw you off balance, drip water all over someone or poke them in the eye. It's curious that someone hasn't invented a better umbrella. There are all kinds of mousetraps but (to my knowledge) only two types of umbrellas available: the standard one we've used for centuries and the little one that is attached to a beanie-type hat. This latter one isn't that great or you would see more of them.

I have an idea for an umbrella. It will have a propeller like a helicopter and it will lift me about 30 feet above the crowd, where I can swoop and glide and be incredibly graceful. I'm calling it my Mary Poppins

Umbrella but, until I perfect it, I will continue to lurch and bump into people saying *perdón, disculpe,* oops! *Lo siento.*

The Peace Corps is Alive and Well in Costa Rica.

It is a surprise to many people who thought this estimable organization had, some years ago, packed up its good works and left the country. It didn't; but about four years ago during a time when the Peace Corps was feeling a financial crunch, it was decided that Costa Rica, along with Chile and Uruguay, was not as much in need of the Peace Corps presence as other countries in this part of the world. However, members of the Peace Corps continued to stay and work with PANI (*Patronato Nacional de Infancia*) to help children, young people, and families at risk. PANI had asked them to stay and keep doing what they were doing, and even gave them an office from which to work.

The Peace Corps presence was increased when officials of the organization ventured beyond the Central Valley to check out some of the villages. There they found that plenty of help could be used. There are now fifty-five volunteers in Costa Rica. They continue their work with street children, but their main concern is rural community development, which includes education, helping local people create projects to generate income, preventing problems by working on self-esteem with children, and creating a parenting skills manual. Although they also find themselves teaching English, this is not what they're about.

Two of my dearest friends, Bonnie and Arnold Hano, were Peace Corps volunteers in Costa Rica in the early 90s. They were in their sixties and more or less retired, Arnold as a writer and Bonnie as a marriage counselor. I met Arnold and Bonnie in a restaurant that used to be in the Omni building. This white-haired gentleman came over to my table and asked me if I was a North American, and would I like to join them for dessert.

We have been fast friends ever since.

Recently I asked Bonnie about their Peace Corps work here. After three months of training in language, culture and methodology, they went off to Turrujal de Acosta, a small community in the mountains about an hour by bus from San José. They were supposed to help with community development. Because they were a couple, they rented a tiny house where they became acquainted with more crawling and flying things than I ever care to know. Their big project was the renovation of the dilapidated elementary school, which was suffering from neglect and earthquake damage. Together they managed to raise $6,000 from their friends in the States, got Protecto to donate 44 gallons of paint, and the parents to contribute labor. The government chimed in with a program they have for paying low-income people for their public works.

Arnold started a girls' volleyball team that is competing to this day. Bonnie started a women's group that resulted in big successes, one woman going back to school to get her high school diploma, another leaving her abusive husband, a third studying to be a nurse and now working at a hospital. They tried to help a struggling women's marmalade co-op; their main contribution was getting them to elect new officers regularly, which was a great improvement.

They also painted a huge moveable map of the world that continues to be used today in the schools. During their two years' stay they attended hundreds of baby showers, birthdays, *novenas*, christenings, and bingo games, and "we drank a lot of beer and listened to a lot of too-loud music," as Bonnie says. They also developed lasting friendships and, after their stint was over, built a charming little house in Turrujal where they spent part of each year during the nineties and attended still more showers, birthdays, *novenas*, christenings, etc.

That may give you an idea of what Peace Corps volunteers do. Just writing about it has exhausted me. For good reason, the Peace Corps slogan is "The toughest job you will ever love." The Hanos shake their heads in dissent. "The toughest job was going home," says Arnold.

Grandma Prudence Goes to School

Not long ago I had the opportunity to visit a country school. I went with director/writer Germán Vargas, who wanted to evaluate the effectiveness of his interactive radio *novela, Coco and Rainbow,* as a tool for teaching English to children in rural schools. I was supposed to act like Grandma Prudence, my character in the *novela,* and talk with the students.

We drove southwest from San José into the mountains through a town called *Amelo o Déjelo* ("Love it or Leave it.") and onto a dirt road. We were less than two hours from San José and half a century away.

Germán told me that the schoolteacher walked this steep road every day to and from school. I didn't believe him. As soon as I was introduced to the teacher, I asked her if she did indeed walk that road every day. She assured me she did and that it was no chore except during rainy season. I was humbled. I had stopped teaching English at the Centro Cultural because I didn't like to walk (on cement sidewalks, small incline) when it rained.

The school itself was a three-room affair, two classrooms and a kitchen/cafeteria where students eat a nourishing free lunch every day. I learned that by law a school must be built for every community with at least twenty families.

We listened to a tape of *Coco and Rainbow* that Germán had brought. The students glanced at me from time to time when Grandma Prudence was heard. They were not convinced that she and I were one and the same.

It was when school was over and lunch had been eaten that I got to experience Costa Rican children in the *campo*. They were all hanging out during what we might call recess. A couple of the boys were playing with a deflated soccer ball.

I said, "I know a game we used to play when I was young," and proceeded to teach them "Anti Anti I Over." Instead of a garage roof, we used Germán's van, the roof of which was taller than the children. The boys were stationed on one side with their backs to the edge of the schoolyard (which ended fifteen feet above the dirt road below – and no fence). The girls were with me on the school side. The object of the game was to toss the ball over the roof of the car, calling "Anti Anti I Over!" That's all I could remember of the game, but the children immediately became enthusiastic.

I noticed that if one person caught the ball more than once she would give it to another student to return. And if a boy missed the ball and it went over the edge onto the road below, a child was quick to volunteer to run 100 yards to the driveway and another 100 yards down the dirt road to retrieve the ball. He would then throw it back so that the game could continue without waiting for his return.

I soon realized that in their enthusiasm for the game the kids were getting their school uniforms dirty (and I was getting tired), so I suggested another game. The rainspout along the rail of the porch emptied into a square of earth boxed by a shallow cement border, which would easily accommodate the soccer ball. I explained what we were going to do: line up and take turns throwing the ball into the "basket."

Within seconds, they formed an orderly line, a mark was made behind which they were to throw, and two girls posted themselves at the basket ready to retrieve and return the ball to the next player. Applause met the successful baskets and moans of sympathy followed the misses. I taught them the English word "almost" to replace the moans at the misses. There was no pushing, no shoving, no complaints when the younger children stood in front of the marker. Nobody suggested points for the successful hoopers, no one suggested teams or winners and losers. Cooperation was writ large, and I got a flash of one of the consequences of 50 years of peace, and realized that Costa Ricans work at it from a very early age.

But the next wave of students for the afternoon classes was coming and this batch had to leave. As they went running down the driveway to the dirt road (how far did THEY have to walk, I wondered), they each turned and waved and called out, "Goodbye, Grandma Prudence!"

"Goodbye, friends," I called, just as I had done so many times on the radio.

Becoming a Resident Changes Your Outlook

My least favorite Spanish word is *trámite* (bureaucratic procedure). Nobody can tell me that "traumatic" isn't a true cognate of that word. I even like the word *basura* (garbage) better. I dread red tape and bureaucracy and long lines to such an extent that for eight years I preferred being a tourist and having to leave this country periodically, or pay the fine for overstaying my tourist visa. It seemed easier than taking the necessary steps to become a resident.

All that has changed. Last August I started the process. With the help of my friend Jerry and the lawyer for the Association of Residents of Costa Rica (ARCR), Lilliana Torres Murillo, I managed to get through the process without once getting frustrated, annoyed or waiting in interminable lines. And this month, there I was, going to Immigration, where a lovely woman presented me with my *carné* and congratulated me with a smile.

I thought that the only change would be not having to worry about leaving the country every three months. Instead my whole world seemed to change. When I walked downtown I saw the city differently. I was personally pleased at the cleanliness of some of the streets and clucked over the ones that weren't so clean, thinking, "Shame on us."

I took pride in every newly painted building. I bought the day's edition of *La Nación* and moved my 501 SPANISH VERBS from the hall bookcase to the mini-library in my bathroom. For the first time, I stopped in the neighborhood *pulpería* (small grocery store) and bought something – potatoes. I started turning on Channel 7 to watch the local news a couple of mornings a week.

I stopped at the *Caja* (social security building) on Avenida 2 to see about getting a *ciudadano de oro* ("golden age" card). It took about ten minutes for them to put me into their computer and tell me to return in twenty-two days for my card.

My next big step was to see about health insurance through the *Caja* – from all I'd heard, the most *"tramitized"* institution in the country. The helpful receptionist there told me to go by my neighborhood clinic and get a card and then return. She wrote down the instructions for me.

My neighborhood clinic is *Carlos Duran*, about twelve blocks from my apartment. I arrived at 1 p.m. and took a number – 53. On the wall above the *ficha* machine was a sign that could have had my name on it. It was addressed to foreigners and said, in effect, "We close at 3 p.m., no matter what." Most of the chairs were occupied and number 30 was being served. I decided to return at sight o'clock the next morning.

Next morning I was dismayed to see the waiting room filled with people, mainly women and children, but soon realized they were there either for appointments or to get rubella shots, thanks to a country-wide campaign. This time I was number 19 and they were serving number 12.

I swear the hands of my watch were moving twice as fast as my perceived time. In what seemed no time at all my number was called and a mere lad, who looked far too young to take care of the matter, took care of the matter by giving me a temporary card and telling me to take it back to the *Caja*.

I crossed the street to the bus stop. I had begun to notice how many buses have signs indicating at which clinics they stop. A woman at the bus stop asked me if the bus stopped at the courts. I told her that the Barrio Lujan bus did, and then I added some silliness about the joys of riding the bus.

"Oh, I didn't realize you were a foreigner," she said. I wanted to say, "I'm not really. I'm a resident." But I resisted.

Once again at the *Caja* I was told to go to window number one for *aseguros voluntarios* (voluntary insurance). Window number one was a whole room filled with people.

I picked number 32 and noted that number seven was being served. The *Caja* is right downtown, so I took my *ficha* number and left. I filled a prescription at the pharmacy, took some money out of my bank's automated teller machine and peeked into a thrift store.

When I returned to the *Caja*, number 30 was being served. Within five minutes another juvenile was asking me questions and filling out an application called *inscripción aseguros voluntarios.* He told me to return on Monday to make my first payment.

Monday morning I arrived before they opened, so I joined the queue waiting to get in. By now I am docilely waiting in all lines. Long ago and far away is the day at the bank when I was so annoyed at the long wait that finally in my exasperation I turned to the woman behind me and asked, "Don't you ever protest the long wait in this bank?" And she replied, "No, but you can. You're from the United States."

Once we entered the building and were directed to our various windows (there are people posted everywhere to direct and help you along), I found myself 23rd in line. Yet within twelve minutes I had paid for two months of health insurance and was on my way, a bona fide voluntarily insured resident.

The next morning, a Friday, I looked fondly at the card my clinic had given me, then looked again. It was a temporary card. The expiration date was that very day. I just couldn't expire on my first day! I gathered together all the papers I had been given, especially the receipts of payment, and hurried the twelve blocks to my clinic.

I pulled out *ficha* number 89. Number 63 was being served. A nice helper asked me what I needed to do. I explained my situation and he went in search of an answer, returning to tell me that I needed to bring in proof of my address. I headed back home. Halfway there I thought that if I hurried, perhaps I could get back before my number was called.

For the first time since I have lived in my apartment, I climbed the 100-meter hill without stopping once and ran up to my third-floor apartment, still without stopping. I grabbed some bills with my address and headed back, taking a shortcut that was also uphill.

I hurried into the clinic, very proud of myself, but also wondering where my neighborhood emergency hospital might be. They were serving number 85. I had barely lowered myself into a seat when my number was called – 86 and 87 evidently hadn't made it back.

In three minutes I had my permanent card – permanent at least until 2003. I took a bus downtown, bought my first Costa Rican pastry, and took another bus home to enjoy it with a cup of very good Costa Rican coffee. It is very good, I thought, to face our fears. So often they are baseless. *Tramites* are not really so frightening.

Renewing my Residency, 2003

This month I had to renew my residency, so the other day I gathered all the papers I thought necessary (a year's report on all the money I had changed into colones, my passport and *carné*) and took a bus downtown and then walked to the Alajuela bus stop. I asked the driver to please tell me when we arrived at Immigration. Then I settled in my seat, pulled out my book and thought how lucky I had been so far – both buses were there when I needed them, no waiting. It was 2:00 p.m., so I figured I had plenty of time. When I looked up from my book and saw a sign that said Airport 9 km, I turned to the man next to me and asked if we had passed Immigration. He said it was way back; everyone in the bus agreed. I knew that. I had been to Immigration before; I just wasn't paying attention and the bus driver had forgotten me.

Everyone began giving me advice. It was agreed that I should get off at the airport and catch a bus back. I did that, and got off at the stop just past Immigration, but on the wrong side of the highway, of course. In order to cross the highway I had to walk two blocks and climb three flights of stairs to the overpass. When I got to the overpass

I lost heart. The stairs had no risers, which meant I could see space and I wasn't sure my acrophobia could handle going up three flights. My mind flashed back to when I was a kid and had to go down to the cellar. Those steps had no risers either, and I was sure that one of the ogres who normally lived under the bridge would grab my leg and pull me through. The fact that I couldn't have fit through that space did not alter my perception of the danger. I returned to the bus stop, and then I decided I wasn't going to let a childhood trauma control me. "Damn it, I can do it," I said.

I almost couldn't. I knew I shouldn't look down, but the cement steps were chipped away in places. I slowly ascended, clinging to the railing, hating the teenagers racing up without a thought. Grimly I walked (in the very middle) across the bridge to the other side. The chain-link fence helped. Then followed the trek back to Immigration. It was about eight blocks, all of which I trudged doggedly. When I saw two men in a little entrance shed, behind a gate, I asked if Immigration was near. One of them said, it was next door, but to get to it I had to go back a block and go around two more blocks. I was beginning to despair. He looked at his watch. "But it is closed anyway." He said. "Closed?" I asked.

"Yes, it closes at 3:30."

I looked at my watch. It was 3:35. "Oh, of course," I said, and started to laugh at the farcical turn of events. But my merriment was short-lived. The second haha stuck in my throat and came out as a sob. Tears began to flow. Horrified, I knew I was about to embark on a case of hysterics. I haven't had hysterics since I was given two traffic violation tickets when I first arrived in California (having driven from Florida). One was for speeding and the other for going too slow. That started out hilarious, too.

With great effort I controlled myself, but the tears wouldn't stop. "Is there a bus stop near by?" I asked. They informed me that the bus stop was in front of the entrance to the Immigration building. That meant another six blocks.

"Isn't there another way?"

Taking pity on me, one of the men opened the gate and led me through the yard – it was a good two blocks – to the back gate, which opened to within two blocks of the bus stop. Closer at hand was a taxi. I had had enough; I told the *taxista* to drop me at the *Gran Hotel*. I should have known, I thought: it always takes me three trips to accomplish any *trámites* in Costa Rica. As I came back from the hotel ladies' room, I stopped at the roulette wheel. Knowing it was not a good idea, I sat down. An hour later I had won ¢5000 and went home, feeling the day had not been a total loss. And I would try again tomorrow.

The Continuing Saga of my Residency Renewal

Whenever I have to get involved in local red tape, I consult with Lynda, who I consider a *trámites* guru. So when I set out a second time to renew my residency, I called her. She wasn't at home, but I remembered that she had said something about going to the ICT in the Post Office. I was covering all bases, so I went there first, starting out at 11:00 a.m. They told me I had to go to Immigration, but there was a blue bus that would take me right to the door; however, they would not recommend that I go to the bus stop because it was in a bad part of the city. So once again I walked to the Alajuela bus. I decided to keep my own eye out for the overhead bridge, at which point I would buzz the driver. It was a very short ride. The walk to the entrance of Immigration was discouragingly long (but not the eight blocks I had thought). I wondered if the new entrance was to discourage the faint-hearted, who would find it easier just to head for the border.

Posted outside the building were "helpers" (that is what I call them), one of whom asked what my intention was and then took me to where I could buy the necessary stamps. Stamps are needed for every *trámite* in Costa Rica. They are never very expensive, but there are so many that they must represent a sizeable income for the government. Once inside the building, I still had to walk the entire length of it to get to the Office for *Pensionados*. Ironically, it was just a few feet away from what used to be the entrance to the building.

But the good news was that there was a very short line and I was served in no time at all. Because my passport was a replacement for the one that was stolen, I had to take it to another desk to get my entrance date verified. While I was waiting at the window, a lovely young woman said hello in a very friendly way. I responded, but she said, "You don't remember me, do you?" I had to admit I didn't. She told me she was the person who had renewed my residency two years before at the other office. At first I was embarrassed, but I realized that there are many very pretty Ticas but few white-haired gringas.

At the window where I had to fill out another form and retrieve my passport, I was told to come back the next day at 1:30. Of course, that magic number of three was going to be fulfilled. On my way out, it dawned on me that I might need some cash to pay for my renewal so I stopped at the information window. He didn't know and suggested I return to the office and ask. There they told me, no, I only needed some stamps (which I had, thanks to the helper).

This time I caught a blue bus that was waiting and got off on Paseo Colón and then made my way home, feeling pretty good.

The next day I decided to have lunch at my favorite sandwich place, Quiznos, on Paseo Colón, and catch the blue bus there. After discovering there were blue buses not going to Immigration, I caught a cab (being a North American I am compulsive about being on time). After picking up my official papers I was on my way home when I realized I still had an expired *carné*. No one had told me what to do about that and I had neglected to ask.

The following day (my fourth visit), I waited in the *Pensionado* office empty of any official. After forty-five minutes I asked the young man waiting next to me if he could help me with some information. He was a treasure trove and informed me that I had to deposit $100 in the Banco Credito Agricola de Cartago, and then come back with two photos and another stamp. I trudged back to the bus.

The next day I decided I would think about it tomorrow.

Still Renewing My Residency

For the average person who does not have a phobia about *trámites,* completing his/her residency renewal would probably take three visits, at the most. For me, I set up a self-fulfilling prophecy – anything that can go wrong will.

However, my fifth visit to Immigration was pretty painless. My friend Sandy, who was visiting from Tilarán, gave me a lift right to the door. I had my receipt for the $100 deposit and I was told I could get the necessary photos right there, which I did. I simply delivered all of this to the proper office and was told to come back in two days to pick up my new *carné*. I also picked up a list of requirements to become a permanent resident. There are no fewer than thirteen steps that must be completed. Not all of them apply to everyone, but even those that didn't apply to me intimidated me. Just think if I had to get all those documents!

Two days hence was a Friday. I decided to give them the benefit of time and waited until Monday to return.

Waiting for someone to appear in the office, I chatted with the other woman there. I'll call her Rachel. She was fluent in both Spanish and English. She told me the person in charge was off looking for her file. She then went into a small tirade about the difficulties she had been having getting her permanent residency. None of the people who were supposed to be in charge seemed to know the rules, because they kept changing. My heart sank.

Two more people joined us, one of them the kind woman who had helped me when I first got my residency. She remembered both my names, and I couldn't remember hers so I'll call her Ariel. She knew Rachel, too, and asked after her family. Then she heard the exasperated story of Rachel's difficulties, which dismayed me all over again.

After Rachel left, Ariel said, "*Rachel se pone muy brava.*" (Rachel gets very angry.) But then, she said that Rachel was Nica (Nicaraguan). This was not a put-down, just a fact. I believe that growing up in a country that is at war, or violent in a major way, makes its people prepared to fight. I said, "But Ticos don't get angry"

"No," She shrugged. "*¿Qué vale?*" (I interpreted this as "To what purpose?")

I smiled and said, "That is one reason I am in Costa Rica." This conversation took place after I had given the woman behind the desk my papers and explained that I had simply come to pick up my *carné,* and she had gone to get it. The woman returned empty-handed and told me I would have to come back tomorrow because it had not been signed yet.

"But," I said, "You told me it would be ready in two days and I waited three!" She shrugged helplessly. "It takes me hours to get here; I have to take three buses." (Bureaucrats are not in the least interested in the trouble we have arriving to stand in front of their desks.) I could feel myself getting really *brava.*

I ranted on, trying to control my ranting because Ariel was being very, very quiet. I could imagine her saying, *"Josefina es muy brava,"* and then explaining – *"Es estadounidense."* Finally, defeated, I asked for a phone number I could call before I came in again, just to make sure my *carné* was indeed ready. She wrote down a number for me. I knew I wouldn't call. If I did, the person on the other end of the line probably wouldn't understand what I was talking about, and if she did know, I probably wouldn't understand what she was talking about. I nodded sheepishly to Ariel and left.

Semana Santa is coming up. I will wait until after that to retrieve my *carné*, hoping it doesn't get lost in the meantime.   I am beginning to think it would be easier for me to become a resident of the Vatican.

The Transition from Tourist to Resident

Living in a foreign country, as opposed to visiting it, is something like getting married after dating someone you love who is trying to impress you. Instead of total acceptance, you start seeing all the warts and idiosyncrasies that are less than perfect, even annoying. But you also become aware of the enduring positive traits. This is what I wrote in my journal after living here just a month. This triggered thoughts about some of the changes that I have noticed.

I am more aware of the increasing crime, especially the increase in violent crime, and am not very happy about this. But I am also pleased that almost nobody hates Costa Rica, because the only time Costa Rica has invaded another country was when its army helped to chase William Walker out of Central America. It has not tried to influence another country except through diplomacy or by its example.

My perception of the country has changed, but so have the priorities of this tourist-*cum*-resident. I was thinking about this the other day as I was walking downtown and saw some tourists with their backpacks and skimpy clothing. Some of them looked as if on safari. San José is a temperate, breezy city. I was wearing long sleeves and slacks and, because it is a city, I wouldn't think of wearing shorts. Of course, there are other reasons why I wouldn't wear shorts. But I do try to look presentable when I go downtown. When I first visited Costa Rica in the late 80's, I bought three pairs of black pumps (about all they had in the shoe stores) because I was embarrassed wearing sandals in the city! Now, when I am not wearing sandals, I wear sneakers, just like the locals.

Instead of waking up to some new experience every day, I have developed a comfortable (and somewhat repetitive) living routine. *Ferias* have replaced *fiestas.* I take as much pleasure in finding the most delicious canned tuna (Sardimar's tuna in olive oil) to eat at home as I did in finding an especially good restaurant.

Instead of going in search of *Quetzals*, I delight in the little sparrows and occasional *Yigüirro* who enjoy the seeds I've put out on the balcony, and I shoo away the bigger greedy pea-headed birds who bully the sparrows. I did see a *Quetzal* once, in Monteverde, I think it was.

When I was just visiting, I thought Costa Rica had some of the handsomest men in the world. Now I notice (and envy) the lovely small-boned long-waisted Ticas and am determined once again to go on a diet. The handsome men must have emigrated.

Instead of looking for a rain forest to tread, I make a little detour in San José to the Parque de España in front of the INS building when I want to experience the peace of a mini rain forest.

I no longer enjoy the weather here as a respite from the less than perfect weather "back home"; I now consider myself lucky for having moved to a place where the coming Ice Age (which I am convinced is what the temperate zones are experiencing), will affect me less.

As a tourist, I ignored the news of the rest of the world. I didn't bother to read newspapers (except for restaurant reviews or local news) and avoided TV. I needed a respite from that, too. Now, as a resident, I am much more involved with what is happening in the rest of the world. I attended the anti-war rally here in San José on Saturday. I was dismayed to learn from a friend's email that in New York not enough room was allowed for the great number of peace demonstrators, and when people tried to join the rally, the police, in an effort to contain the frustrated people, ran their horses into the crowd. Here, at our demonstration that filled the *plaza* in front of the Teatro Nacional, I didn't see one member of the police force. Of course, none was needed. There were plenty of people but no one expected any problems, and there weren't any.

Rule Number Four

As a going away present when I left San Jose, California, a friend gave me *Life's Little Instruction Book* with 511 suggestions and advice on "how to live a happy and rewarding life."

If I were to write my own instruction book for San José, Costa Rica, "Learn Spanish" would be Rule Number One. My book would also include "Don't slam taxi cab doors." If you do, you will see a rolling of eyes heavenward and hear *sotto voce* muttering with the audible word "*gringo*" on the order of, "Just because you rich *gringos* have big cars with heavy doors, doesn't mean we do."

Number Three would be, "Don't leave home without a book." A book comes in very handy when you are tired of people-watching while waiting in line or riding a bus. I have doubled the number of books I normally read and also reduced my frustration noticeably.

Which brings me to Rule Number Four (perhaps the most important of all), "Don't lose your temper." Getting mad in Costa Rica is simply not done. It goes against their peaceful coexistence code and it won't do you any good anyway. I have seen a bank teller simply turn away from an irate foreigner who is ranting about something or other. I keep learning this lesson over and over.

Not long ago I walked from Muñoz y Nanne, a supermarket, to the Banco de Costa Rica in San Pedro. This is not a long walk, but I was carrying two heavy bags of groceries. After I had deposited a check in my dollar account, I looked at the balance and thought it was less than it should be. I questioned the teller, who told me I needed to ask a desk person. So I went over to where the bank clerks were, took a *ficha* and waited my turn. As I sat there I thought, "Oh, lord, I hope he doesn't ask for an I.D." because I didn't have any with me. I don't like to carry my passport unless I know I am going to need it. I don't have a driver's license. There were enough signs around to let me know I needed an I.D.

Rather quickly my number was called and I was sitting at the desk behind which was a nice looking, stocky young man with glasses who asked how he could help me. I told him I wanted to know the balance in my dollar account and shoved my savings account card under the glass partition at him. He opened it, looked at it. "May I have your identification, please," he asked.

"I don't have it with me," I said. "But I just want you to look at my account and tell me why it is $200 short. I don't want to take any money out."

81

"I'm sorry," he smiled politely. "But I need some form of identification."

"All I want is that *you* look at my account." That is how I started my response, but somehow from there it escalated into a tirade that ended with something sarcastic like, "You can look at me and see I am not who I say I am, but in truth I am a thief who is here to trick you and rob this bank!"

He, of course, was dumbfounded by my outburst. He didn't know I had carried two heavy bags of groceries four blocks or that I hadn't had lunch and it would take me an hour to go home and come back again.

He simply handed me my card. I grabbed it and my sacks of groceries, stormed out of the bank, and stomped down the street, my adrenalin high. Half a block away I stopped and realized what I had done. I was going to live the rest of the day feeling rotten about how I had acted. And that poor young man would have another story of an ugly North American to talk about, not to mention how upset he must be. Nobody likes to be yelled at – least of all a Tico. I turned around and lugged my bags of groceries back to the bank. I took another *ficha* and sat down and waited. I refused the two other desks when they became free. The customer ahead of me at "my desk" took so long he must have been getting a loan to buy a house, but I was glad; I needed a bit of penance.

After twenty more minutes my number was called. The stocky young man with glasses visibly flinched when he saw me, but he managed to ask what he could do for me. I immediately explained that I did not want him to do anything, I wanted to apologize for my behavior. It came out something like, "Excuse me for being so badly brought up. I know the rules and that you must follow them." When I took a breath he said, "May I have your bank card please?"

Each time he said that, I repeated myself, adding, "No, No, I didn't come back to have you do anything, I just want to say I am sorry. Please excuse me."

"Please," he said. "Give me your card." Finally I did. He checked my account and found my error and explained it to me. He gave me back my card with a smile. I out-smiled him, thanked him profusely and told him he was very kind indeed, and left, practically swinging my bags. I felt infinitely better that he could go home, still liking his job, with no new story about awful gringas.

Which brings me to Rule Number 5: If you've screwed up on some of the others, an apology can't hurt.

Tico Sayings

The past week has seen the return of typical summer weather. At last, after an unusually cold Christmas season and changeable weather into January, we are now enjoying warm sunny days with blue skies and a cool breeze. The clouds gather in the afternoon, making for chilly evenings.

My friend Sandy came in from Tilarán for the Pavarotti concert. It was held in the large soccer stadium in *La Sabana*. She said she was almost freezing, and so far away from the stage that even her binoculars weren't much help seeing the legendary tenor. But there were huge screens and it was all worth it.

This week I acquired a new maid (*empleada*) after months of trying to keep my apartment clean myself, and failing so miserably that the bottoms of my socks are black in no time. Her name is Socorro – which is very fitting because I was in need of help. So today I was able to sit on my balcony in the sun and read (after showing her the ropes and doing some work myself).

Someone sent me some *Tico* sayings. Typical sayings tell you something about a people – usually their ability to make fun of the less admirable traits they have. Or sometimes they just tell a universal truth. So, here is a Spanish lesson of *Tico* sayings:

Tener la conciencia limpia es síntoma de mala memoria.
A clean conscience is a symptom of a bad memory.

Pez que lucha contra la corriente, muere electrocutado.
Fish that fight against the current get electrocuted.

La esclavitud no se abolió, se cambia a ocho horas diarias.
Slavery has not been abolished; it changed to eight hours a day.

Si la montaña viene hacia ti... Corre, es un derrumbe.
If the mountain comes to you, run, it's a landslide.

No soy un completo inútil. . . Por lo menos sirvo de mal ejemplo.
I'm not completely useless. At least I serve as a bad example.

Errar es humano, pero echarle la culpa a otro es más humano todavía.
To err is human, but to blame somebody else is even more so.

Huya de las tentaciones—despacio, para que puedan alcanzarte.
Run from temptations—slowly, so that they can catch you.

Estudiar es desconfiar de la inteligencia del compañero al lado.

To study is to not have confidence in the student next to you.

La mujer que no tiene suerte con los hombres no sabe la suerte que tiene.
Women who don't have luck with men don't know how lucky they are.

La pereza es la madre de todos los vicios, y como madre hay que respetarla.
Laziness is the mother of all vices, and as a mother it should be respected.

Trabajar nunca mata a nadie. . . pero ¿para qué arriesgarse?
Work never killed anybody—but why risk it?

Hay dos palabras que te abrirán muchas puertas: "Jale y Empuje".
There are two words that open many doors: "Pull and Push."

In the case of my balcony door, the word is "slide." Socorro and I agreed that next time she will get rid of all the dead plants on my balcony and from now on I will have artificial or dried plants and flowers. After she left, I padded around my apartment, enjoying the neatness and the feel of clean tiles. Checking the bottoms of my socks, I discovered them still pretty clean. Socorro is a keeper.

Parsing "To Serve" and "To Help" in Costa Rica

I am not entirely Pollyanna in *Pura Vida* Land; I do have a pet peeve regarding the Costa Rican interpretation of service. It seems to fall at two extremes: either it is, "I'll take care of you as soon as I finish this conversation with my fellow worker," or the clerk comes rushing up to you almost before you get in the door to ask, "May I help you?"

The first response usually occurs in banks and offices, the latter in stores. It's the rapid-response type that annoys me most. Unless I am filling a prescription in a *farmacia*, I usually don't know exactly what I want; I just want to look, damn it. Each time that happens, my temperature goes up, especially in a thrift store.

Sometimes when hit with that question, I have replied, "Perhaps, what do you have?" Of course, the response is usually a smile and a shrug and, "Well, this is a *Ropa Americana...*" so I smile back and say, "Of course, so I will just look around." And she backs off – slightly.

These incidents have made me think of the larger question of what constitutes good service. When Costa Rica was first becoming a popular tourist destination, there was a concern that Ticos were not finely attuned to the concept of service, so necessary to attract tourists.

One explanation was that, during the Colonial era in Costa Rica, in spite of an underclass of servants and even slaves, the opposite condition – egalitarianism – managed to co-exist. This has continued to this day, along with the belief in the essential dignity and equality of every individual. All of this could add up to a people who are happy to help, but not too willing to serve.

Thinking about this made me look up "serve" and "help" in the dictionary. As one can imagine, there are many definitions, especially of "serve," but the first definition is, "to work for as a servant," and is derived from the words for slave, servant and serf. "Help," on the other hand, means "to make things easier or better for a person, to aid, assist." Thinking about these definitions, it seemed to me that Costa Ricans know the difference very well.

What in other countries are considered "household servants" here are called *empleadas*.

However, I have decided that super-attentiveness is neither good service nor is it very helpful, and each time it happens, I get more annoyed. So I was prepared the other day when I walked into a thrift store on the Paseo de los Estudiantes and the girl rushed up to me and asked, "May I help you with something?"

Full of mock pleasantness, I replied, "Yes, you can. I am looking for a long-sleeved green blouse. Do you have one?"

"Follow me," was her sincerely pleasant response. I followed her into the back room where, from a long rack of blouses, she pulled a long-sleeved green blouse and handed it to me. I was busy swallowing my gall, but I managed to croak, "I don't think I like that shade of green." She then took a backward step and pulled out a long-sleeved T-shirt in a slightly different color. It was (thankfully) a size six so I could reject it.

I wasn't ready to concede, but I was able to smile regretfully and say, "I'll just look around a bit on my own." She nodded, still pleasant, but she didn't leave the room. (Now I understand this hovering is motivated by the desire to prevent shoplifting.) Finally I shrugged and started to go.

"There are more blouses in the back room. Perhaps there is what you want."

I went into the back-back room and just happened to find a blue-green long-sleeved silk blouse that fit perfectly.

Upon leaving I thanked her and added, since I couldn't think of the word for helpful, "*Era muy, er, ah, muy amable,*" falling back on the standard phrase all Ticos use.

Once home I looked up the word "helpful" in my *Compact Spanish and English Dictionary, Second Edition.*

I had to smile. The Spanish word for helpful was *amable.* Obviously being helpful is valued here. As for me, I wondered once again, when I was going to let Ticos be Ticos?

Pet Peeves

Being out of touch with the pulse of the United States, I don't know what the current pet peeves of U.S. Americans are but, thanks to my friend Jerry, I have a list of things that annoy Ticos. A lot of them seem to be connected to modern technology and the proliferation of cars on the streets. It is not hard to identify with the annoyed or the annoyer. Here are some of the pet peeves Ticos have:

Drivers who have their radios at full volume.

Women who wear short-short mini-skirts and then keep tugging them down.

People who ostentatiously put their cellular phones on the table in a restaurant.

Parents who give cell phones to children under 15 to take to school. (Apropos of this, I remember a teacher telling me that one of her third-graders with a cell phone called home and said, "Mami, come get me, the teacher was mean to me.")

People who pay for purchases under ¢1000 (about $3.00) with a credit card.

People who sell avocados on the street, displaying a cut one that is perfect, and you discover a bag full of rotten ones when you get home.

The fat doctor who urges you to diet.

People in fast food restaurants who order a super hamburger, large fries and a diet soft drink.

People who eat fried chicken on the bus.

People who go into a Chinese restaurant and order a hamburger.

Women who carry little dogs that are all dressed up like dolls, then keep kissing them.

Drivers who honk a nanosecond after the light has turned green (actually, this is the *definition* of a nanosecond in Costa Rica).

Those who move before the light has turned.

Parents who say their seven-year-old is an expert at navigating the Internet, even if it's true.

Drivers who park in spaces reserved for the disabled.

People who take advantage of their *ciudadano de oro* cards to get privileges like getting in front of others in lines at the bank, etc. (Oops, up until now my record was clear.)

Right now my pet peeve is having an appointment with someone for 9 a.m., and then being told they will be two hours late because their car is in the shop and it won't be ready until eleven, and you know that when they call the mechanic, they will be told that their car won't be ready till one, and so on, until you discover you have spent the whole day doing nothing but wait.

The car in the shop is like the computer being down: everything stops.

I am having this problem at the moment because they are going to re-tile my apartment and I have spent two days putting all my possessions into the two rooms that were newly tiled when I moved in. (I had this nightmarish thought that they were going to dig out the old tile before putting in the new. The dust, I thought, would permeate everything. Forever. But I was informed that they simply clean the old and glue the new on top.) This means they have to redo the molding and all the doors because the floor is higher; or put another way, my ceiling is lower. I love high ceilings so much that when I lived in New York I cut down the legs of all my furniture, dining room chairs, table, couch, everything, so my ceiling would seem higher – at least when I was sitting down.

So, with help from my landlord, I moved into a studio apartment he has in San Pedro. He gave me two sets of keys and off he went. I put my stuff away and wrote down all the things I forgot to bring, and fixed myself something to eat. Later, after the rain stopped, I decided to go to the store and COULDN'T FIND MY KEYS! I tore the place apart. Three times. I couldn't leave to find Henry, the caretaker, because the door automatically locked when it closed. I couldn't call anyone because one of the things I hadn't brought was my phone book. I began to feel as if I were in a Hitchcock movie and the plot called for me to eventually jump out the window.

Finally I managed to call my friend Lillian who called Darrylle who called Dannys, the caretaker of the other building, who called Henry, who came upstairs and helped me scour my apartment again – to no avail. It was now 6:30 and I had a dinner date, so we closed the door on a towel to keep it from locking and off I went with his assurances that he would check on my apartment from time to time.

When I got home I had to ring the bell for Henry and he came out smiling. He had found my keys! They were right in the kitchen on the counter where I thought I had put them, but I had put my toaster oven on top of them! Rule number two about finding things: they are usually under something else you have recently set down.

I certainly hope that this happy ending means that the dark bad luck cloud which has been hovering over me for the past month and a half is drifting away, because one of my really big pet peeves is someone who is always complaining.

When in Rome, First Check Things Out

Some people are under the impression that I am an authority on Costa Rica. Anyone who has to make eight visits to Immigration to renew a *cédula* is no expert. (When I use the word *cédula*, I actually am referring to the ID card we are given as residents and that is also called a *carné*.) When it comes to Costa Rica, I paraphrase that popular disclaimer, "I don't know much about this country, but I know what I like." I think that is what people who are considering coming here – especially to live – should think about. What do I like? What is important to me?

Like anywhere in the world, if you have lots of money, you can live here very comfortably, pretty much on your own terms. But you still have values, and a world view and an expectation of people, and it's nice to be in an environment where these are compatible. Often it is the little things that make or unmake your contentment.

I knew there were certain things I wanted in order to be comfortable. I wanted to live where bougainvillea grew (a warm climate); I wanted to be able to drink the water and flush a toilet; I wanted access to some of the things I love – music and theater and good restaurants. I wanted good public transportation because I did not want to own a car – or anything, for that matter.

On a deeper level, I wanted to experience living in a country without an army, without the idea that war is a solution. (Fighting wars are what armies are for.) Not having an army affects the psyche of a people, just as having one does. I come from the United States, where "winning is everything" is a value. One can see this as the war in Iraq keeps grinding on. Here in Costa Rica, it is the morality of war that the people are concerned with, not winning. Except for soccer and politics, having a winner and a loser is not how Ticos think. They want win-win situations. That is one reason they are so careful to avoid confrontations.

Heather, an email friend, recently moved to Costa Rica to work. So far, she loves it here, and her pleasure is enhanced because she is around people who seem to be very happy. She also commented that when her boss gives her a project she assumes he means he wants it right away. He doesn't. He expects it in a week or two, and has told her to slow down. But her creativity flourishes when she is under pressure. Heather is from the U.S.

Her experience reminds me of the story about the anthropologist living with a tribe in New Guinea, I think it was. They were a happy people, but the chief of this small tribe was in possession of the only hatchet. Every day he would lend it to another member of the tribe, who would do whatever job he had to do and return it at the end of the day. Getting caught up in her participant status and wanting to help, the anthropologist sent to the States for a load of hatchets and happily handed them out to everyone in the tribe. The productivity of the people increased considerably, but there was also a breakdown in the social order of the tribe. The rituals and the relationships that had centered on the hatchet were gone. Social chaos ensued. It could be argued that everyone's having a hatchet was far more democratic and productive. But was it the role of the anthropologist to bring about the change without preparing the people for the consequences?

Thinking of the story, I suggested to Heather that she work at her own pace – and then sit on the finished product a while; that perhaps one of the reasons Ticos are happy is that they are not under pressure to do everything yesterday. I have no doubt that Heather will figure out how to stay happy here. For North Americans elsewhere, one can only hope.

Food for Thoughts

The Eternal Debate: Broccoli vs. Chocolate

Now we are in the peaceful time of *Semana Santa,* and the quiet makes me believe I could be in Venice. The traffic has gone to the beaches. I love Easter and Christmas because everyone disappears to the beach. Almost everyone. Some men are painting my building and right now one of them is in my *cuarto de pilas* (open-air laundry room), which is often referred to as simply *pila,* just outside my kitchen. They are removing the flaking paint and making everything a bright yellow.

I am cooking in the kitchen. I keep buying broccoli at the *feria* because I know it is good for me, but I have lost my taste for this member of the cabbage family. Since it is low in calories and high in vitamins, especially A – and there is more A in the leaves, so we should eat them, too – I want to eat more. I have invented a recipe that enables me to eat half a small head of broccoli at one sitting. It is simple and fast. Break the florets into bite sizes, peel stems, steam or boil to your taste of doneness. Meanwhile heat a small frying pan and lift the broccoli out of the water into it, stirring rapidly to remove the water; when the broccoli is dry, add a bit of butter and olive oil and a generous teaspoon or more of roasted garlic, some Jane's Krazy Mixed-Up seasonings and pepper. Toss and eat.

Speaking of cabbage, this vegetable, which is very popular in Costa Rica, is native to the Mediterranean and has been cultivated for about 2500 years. The Roman Cato said that if you plan to eat a lot at a banquet, beforehand you should eat as much cabbage, with a sprinkling of vinegar, as you want, then after dinner, eat a few more leaves and you will feel that you haven't eaten at all. AND you can drink as much as you like. Costa Ricans seem to serve grated cabbage on everything, including hot dogs!

In case you haven't roasted garlic before, simply take three or four bulbs; slice the tops off so the buds are revealed, sprinkle with olive oil, wrap in foil and bake at 350 degrees for about an hour, the last fifteen minutes out of the foil. Then I cut the bottoms and squeeze the roasted garlic into a jar, cover with olive oil. It lasts for weeks in the fridge. I can buy four bulbs of garlic for 100 colones at the *feria*.

Neither of these recipes is typically Costa Rican. Each holiday here seems to have a special typical Costa Rican dish. One is *chiverre*. It is a sweet condiment made from a large squash and it's ubiquitous at Easter time. From what my friends tell me, it is a lot of work so I haven't tried it. But another Easter offering is the *flor de itabo*. Looking at it at the *feria* you would think it is simply a branch of white flowers hanging upside down in some stalls. I took some home and according to instructions from another friend, boiled the flowers briefly and then scrambled them with eggs. They tend to be a bit bitter and I liked the idea more than the experience. I have been told that the uncooked white petals in a salad remind one of endive. They are also boiled with diced potatoes and seasoned with salt and garlic.

After my lunch of mainly broccoli under the eyes of the painters, I decided to enjoy downtown. I went to my favorite store, The Cleveland, on Sixth Avenue, near the church *La Merced*. It is, of course, a *Ropa Americana* store, a place where you can still find blouses and shirts with pockets, albeit used. Over the years I have noticed the interesting phenomenon that the clothes I wear all the time tend to grow with me, (up to a point) but when I try on the same size in a store it is way too small. This was happening with everything I was trying on at the Cleveland. I came home with nothing new and so will share my last bit of cooking news. I have been experimenting with making chocolate candies. I make fudge sauce for ice cream, but I figured some people sometimes want chocolate without having to put it on something. So I started making chocolate candy. I have decided to stop this new enterprise. It is not that it is not good; it is simply that my ability to sample the chocolate sauce is limited once it is in the jars, but with candy I find I am eating two-thirds of every recipe, piece by piece. That is why those clothes weren't fitting. Five cups of shredded cabbage has 24 calories, and a pound of broccoli has 32 calories. One piece of chocolate? Forget it. My culinary future is clear.

Living the Comfy Narrow Life

The truth is, most of us live very narrow lives. With all the choices out there, we tend to make the same ones over and over, never expanding our experiences. (Note: I have Freud's habit of generalizing from observations of myself.) You are free to say, as my friend Betty justifiably can, "That's not my problem, kiddo." But you probably won't.

I was becoming aware of this at the Saturday *feria,* where I saw dozens of fruits and vegetables that are totally unknown to me. But instead of trying something new, I continued to pick out the same ones over and over – tomatoes, celery, strawberries, carrots, grapefruit, pineapple, etc. Occasionally I will buy some spinach, which is not like the spinach one gets in the States. And I have bought *zapallitos.* They are like the good old familiar zucchini, and maybe even better. But that is about the extent of it. I don't even know the names of all that other produce, not to mention how to prepare them.

It is not just with the food that we buy and prepare that we tend to stick to the tried and true. Think about restaurants. How often, when you go out to eat, do you go to the same restaurant and order the same dish? And there are so many new ones opening in San José and environs it would be easy to expand one's repertoire. Speaking of environs, I thought, when I moved to Costa Rica over ten years ago, that it would be a wonderful 'jumping off' place. A home base from which I would visit all the countries I have never been to. Other than trips back to the States, to Panama and Nicaragua, I have been nowhere. I have rarely explored other parts of this country except when friends come to visit.

And how many new friends have you made recently? I am not being accusatory. Actually, these questions are directed at myself. The reason my thoughts have gone in this direction is something I was reading. It was about falling in love. There is a chemical that the body secretes, a chemical called phenylethylamine (PEA) that surges through the nerve cells and affects both our thoughts and our feelings. This chemical makes us feel euphoric, rejuvenated, optimistic and energized – able to leap over tall buildings. All of our senses are heightened. PEA is so pleasurable it is addicting. I knew and wrote about this many years ago, but what I didn't know was that the same chemical (PEA) is secreted when we experience new thrills. And how can we experience new thrills or fall in love if we don't try new things and meet new people? Once in a while two people who have known each other for years suddenly fall in love, but it is rare.

On the other hand, there is another group of chemicals that takes over under different circumstances. They are powerful pain relievers and they calm and reassure us. They are the endorphins that are secreted when we experience intimacy, empathy, dependability and oft-shared experiences. They are responsible for the good feelings that come from stability, friendship and familiarity. As it turns out, they are even more addictive than PEA. So there must be a reason we tend to choose the familiar, hang on to our friends and go back to that restaurant and have that favorite dish: the reason that we crave comfort food and miss our family and avoid the possibility of another heartbreak and more heartburn.

Second-Hand Rose

I love thrift stores and second-hand bookstores. I have friends, and even family, who wouldn't go near either, which started me thinking about why it is that I like them.

Of course, the price is usually right, and I love bargains. I was telling a visiting friend, Marylou, the other night that only in thrift stores and used bookstores can you find real treasures. I said that a treasure is something you find that you love at a bargain price. She took exception to this, saying that a treasure is anything you value beyond price. She was thinking of her daughter, the family photo album and the like. I was thinking of the phrase, "One man's trash is another man's treasure." After looking up "treasure" in Roget's, I decided she was probably more right than I.

But I love thrift stores for other reasons, too. New stores with nothing but new items confine you to the present, to the fashions and tastes of the day. Going into a thrift store I can travel to another decade, I can browse among old friends and find something that suits me better than current fads.

I have always resented that in the U.S. I am described first of all as a consumer when mentioned in the abstract. I don't like the responsibility of having to buy and consume to keep the national economy healthy. I'm not a good consumer.

You can't be a good consumer and recycle, and I love the idea of recycling. (Reincarnation appeals to me for that reason.) I especially like recycled books. I have friends – well, one, and he knows who he is – who is repelled by the thought of handling a used book. Although I feel bad for the author who doesn't make any money on his resold book, I like the idea that someone has enjoyed the book before me and thought enough of it to put it where others might enjoy it. (Although I have recently learned that all of those best-sellers listed in newspapers are not necessarily the most read. People sometimes buy books like they buy other things – because other people have bought them).

Mainly, though, I don't think that what is being published today is better than yesterday or yesteryear. Recently I found *The Disappearance* by Phillip Wylie, a book I have been looking to re-read for two years. After an intensive search I managed to get W. Somerset Maugham's play, *The Constant Wife.* Neither of those two books is available in new bookstores.

Until recently two stores in downtown San José sold used English language books. The one on Avenida de los Estudiantes moved last year and decided to close out its English library. They had dumped the books on the floor so they could take the shelves to their new store, and they told me I could rummage through them.

As much as I love rummaging through bookshelves, this was not a pleasant task. But I found a real treasure for about 25 cents: *Beloved,* written by Vina Delmar in the 1950's, is a beautiful fictional biography of Judah P. Benjamin, a brilliant lawyer and fascinating figure of the Southern Confederacy. This book was originally sold in Costa Rica (perhaps second-hand even then) at the *Casa de las Revistas* in San José. An M. D. Weston thought enough of the book to stamp his or her name in the front. This find has sent me in search of more books by Delmar and about Judah Benjamin.

We still have Mora's Bookstore. I have to smile every time I go in there because I wonder if this is going to be the day that Darin Mora, the ever-pleasant owner, will have completely disappeared behind the stack of books on his counter. Darin has owned Mora Books for six years and before that worked for Book Traders in the same totally inadequate little store with the incredible collection of used books, CDs, and comics. I looked around at the thousands of books on the shelves and on the floor and wondered how many treasures were there, then I asked Darin to keep an eye out for anything by Vina Delmar. He said he would and added that none so far had come in. We both smiled. I believed him, because people in the used book trade know things like that.

Combating the Snarls

When some friends, back from a visit to Florida, mentioned that a medium-sized watermelon was $10 in the supermarket there, which seemed like a lot to me, so I thought it would be interesting to compare the prices of watermelon. I would, I decided, go to the Saturday *feria* (farmers' market) and check out the watermelons.

Saturday didn't start out to be a great day. As my mother used to say, I got up on the wrong side of the bed, or I was at sixes and sevens. Everything was in a snarl. There are enough descriptions of how I felt that make me think it's pretty common. I had offered to make the main dish for a charades get-together at noon, and as soon as I awoke I was regretting my offer.

And although I was up at 6 a.m., my neighbors, who usually give me a lift to the *feria*, were not at home. I just didn't feel like walking the mile or so. But I had my coffee and set off. My mental outlook did not improve, even with walking. I was simply feeling sorry for myself, and nothing was going to change that. I noticed another woman walking across the street a little ahead of me. She obviously was going to the *feria* too because she was pulling a cart. If I kept her in my sights, I couldn't get lost. Sometimes I daydream as I walk and lose my way.

I was thinking about my friend Jerry, and what he had said the other day when he was giving me a lift somewhere. Jerry used to be director of personnel at a university, and I have found people in personnel have an almost knee-jerk response of "How can I help you?" to people who even look as if they could use some help. Jerry is also genuinely a nice guy.

We were discussing the ever-increasing traffic and how maddening it was. He said that when he finds himself especially annoyed with other drivers or with traffic in general, he lowers his annoyance by doing three kind acts. He was telling me this as he braked and waved to the car stuck in the next lane to get in front of us. Usually after the third good deed, he said, he has been thanked so much and feels so good about himself he is no longer annoyed.

I was thinking this when I saw a taxi and I hailed it. As I got in, I asked the taxi driver if he would stop down the street for the woman with the cart. I then called to her and asked if she would like to ride. In a moment we were putting her cart in the back seat while she got in the front of the taxi. At the *feria*, she blessed me enough for three people, and I was beginning to feel a bit better.

There were a number of stands selling watermelons. They must be in season. And the price varied from 100 to 150 colones a kilo. (That's about 15 cents a pound.) Some were halves and they looked delicious, but I wasn't about to carry one home. Instead, I bought four tomatoes, three red peppers, a large cauliflower, a small broccoli, a papaya, a small pineapple, four carrots, a daikon radish, a box of strawberries and a dozen calla lilies. All of this came to approximately $4.90. To be perfectly fair, I should include the cost of two taxis, about $1.30, and admit that in the supermarket watermelons are 170 colones a kilo (still nowhere close to Florida's $10 a melon).

When I got home and was putting everything away, I remembered something else my Florida-visiting friends said: "In Florida we found ourselves eating processed food and a lot more meat, and we realized that we eat so much healthier in Costa Rica." This doesn't mean there are no processed foods here. But it is easier to resist them. Costa Rica also has a lot of "exotic" vegetables and fruits that I never buy simply because they are unfamiliar. That made me think of something T. H. White said in *The Once and Future King*: "When you're sad, learn something new."

Maybe, when you're in a snarl, you should try something new. There is another saying I have – and I made this one up myself: when everything is going wrong you might as well throw a monkey wrench into the mix and see what happens.

Next time, I will buy one strange fruit or vegetable. Trying to figure out what to do with it is both learning something new and throwing a monkey wrench into the situation.

The Incredible Edible Feria Egg

I love eggs. They are delicious and versatile. With eggs you can make *bocas*, (appetizers), a main course or a dessert. They are as crowd-pleasing as deviled eggs and as elegant as zabaglione. They are as complete a food as you can find. One large egg will give you six and a half grams of protein, good amounts of iron, phosphorus, thiamin and Vitamins A, D, E, and K. I am convinced that the cholesterol in an egg is offset by the lecithin that is also found in eggs. Eggs contain the globulin lysozyme (also

105

present in saliva) which weakens the cell walls of bacteria and thus helps reduce the chances of infection. Eggs have had a bad rap.

When I lived in Gettysburg, Pennsylvania, I often stopped by an egg-candling factory on my way to class. I learned the difference between an AA-grade egg and a grade B egg. A doubleA egg has a nice round yolk and a thick murky white that stands up nicely around the yolk. The white of a grade B egg is more transparent and likely to spread all over the frying pan when you crack it, and the yolk is more likely to break. As an egg ages, the white gets more transparent and runnier and the yolk flattens and breaks more easily.

Because eggshells are porous, eggs lose their freshness rapidly. It is best to refrigerate them or coat the shells with mineral oil. A cracked egg, or one that has been opened and is susceptible to bacteria, should be used as soon as possible. You can tell how fresh an egg is by putting it in a pan of cold water. A fresh egg will sit on the bottom of the pan, a not-so-fresh egg will float with its wider end up, and a rotten egg will swim to the top. If you scramble eggs or use them in cooking, the grade is not a problem, but if you like poached eggs, as I do, it is. And therein lies the problem. I have been unable to find AA fresh eggs in Costa Rican markets. Nobody in the supermarkets, and certainly not in the *pulperias*, thinks it is important to refrigerate eggs and they certainly don't oil them.

The *feria,* or farmers' market, closest to me is held on Saturday morning. Last Saturday I woke up thinking, "If the *feria* has fresher fruits and vegetables maybe the egg farmers have just gathered them and they are fresher too." So off I marched at 7:00 a.m. to the Plaza Víquez to test my hypothesis.

106

Walking in San José early in the morning is still a joy. There is little traffic and the few people on the street are coming out of the *panaderías* with long loaves of freshly baked bread that give the streets a European flavor and smell. At the *feria* I went immediately to the egg stands, choosing the stand with the handsome couple and their teenage boys. I decided on extra large white eggs (shell color makes no difference to an egg's nutritional value – I was just tired of brown eggs). I had brought my own container because I never manage to arrive home without at least two broken eggs in the containers the supermarkets provide. I bought some fresh vegetables and fruit and caught a taxi home. I immediately put one of the eggs in a pan of water. It dutifully sat on the bottom of the pan. I hadn't eaten breakfast, so I decided to fry my egg because that way I could tell the grade better. After a glass of freshly squeezed orange juice, I fried a little bacon – I won't discuss the nutritional value of bacon here – and then cracked an extra large white *feria*-bought egg into the frying pan. The nice round yolk sat in the middle of a mound of thick murky white. I like my fried eggs basted so I put a teaspoon of water in the frying pan and covered it. In a few minutes I had a perfect basted egg. I ate it. I sat for a few minutes thinking about how good it was. Then I went back into the kitchen and tried a poached egg. It is best to poach eggs that are cold from the fridge, but egg whites beat best if they are at room temperature.

Beautiful fresh AA grade eggs are worth a Saturday morning walk to the *feria*. Carefully refrigerated (they say you shouldn't keep them in the door, rather you should keep them covered) the other ten should be fresh all week and supremely edible no matter how I decide to prepare them.

Oh yes, I came across the answer to what came first, the chicken or the egg. The egg! Dinosaurs were here before chickens, and they laid eggs, although I'm not sure I'd like to eat one.

More Reasons for Shopping at the Feria

The world doesn't seem to be getting better. With fear and depression – both economic and personal – hovering over everyone, many are looking for somewhere where they can live a safe, simple, stress-less and affordable life. I know of no place in the world that fills that bill completely. Back in the sixties I found Majorca, Spain, and moved my family there. We lived for three good years on that lovely island. Now I don't think I could afford three *weeks* in Majorca.

Costa Rica has filled some of these requirements for me. It is probably as safe from terrorist attacks as any place in the world. Foreign terrorists, that is. Costa Rica has its own crime problem. When I first moved here, some *Nica* "terrorists" occupied the Nicaraguan Embassy and took the people inside hostage. While in there, they used a computer to make a big sign that they hung in the window. It said in Spanish, "We're Sorry, Costa Rica." I can't imagine that happening today.

One can certainly get back to the simple life in Costa Rica – and I mean basic; you can find places on remote unpaved roads without electricity or indoor plumbing. That is living at its cheapest, but don't ask me where to find them, please. Stress free? Well, most of us make our own stress – with considerable help from the jobs we hold. But if you are able to quit your job, or are about to retire, I think Costa Rica, even with its own brand of stresses, is as good as it gets. Mind you, if I could afford it, I would probably opt for at least half of every year in Italy. Between the Italian view of life and their love of good food, I think I could happily fit in. But the catch is "affordable."

The *comida típica* of Costa Rica, which usually includes rice, beans, cabbage, and plantains, cannot compete with the cuisine of Italy, but it is, in fact, a pretty healthy diet and can be obtained quite cheaply. Besides, Costa Rica offers a great variety of fruits and vegetables at reasonable prices. And just about every week a new restaurant opens featuring foreign cuisine (including Italian).

Thinking of affordable good food and a stress less way to shop, I decided to price the produce I generally buy at the local *feria*. Then I asked Laureen Diephof, who writes a consumer column for a California newspaper, to price the same things there. This particular Saturday I bought 6 extra-large eggs, 64¢; 6 grapefruit (grapefruit here have lots of seeds), 51¢; a liter of freshly squeezed orange juice, 90¢; 4 hearts of romaine (1/2 kilo), 51¢; 2 cartons of not great strawberries, $1.28; 1 lb. local apples 70¢; 1 lb. miniature squash and zucchini, 90¢; 1 miniature cauliflower, 26¢; 1 small pineapple, 77¢; 1 kilo (4 large) tomatoes that still taste like tomatoes, $1.03; 4 ears of sweet corn, (these, I believe, are imported, although corn is available here) $1.15; and a bunch of 13 small bananas, 26¢. The total came to $8.75.

Laureen shopped for the same things, but in a supermarket, so we must make allowances. Her purchases totaled $29.47. Now I am sure everything she bought was washed and packaged and free of blemishes. That is not so here. Her largest expense, surprisingly, was the cheapest here – the grapefruit.

Although a vegetarian or fruitarian could eat more cheaply, one can find a good selection of meat and fish and seafood, too. The price of fish and seafood was very reasonable when I moved here but has since skyrocketed now that most of it is being exported. The same thing has happened with flowers, but they are much cheaper at the *feria*. A vase full of flowers on my coffee table adds luxury to my apartment, and looking at them gives me pleasure – especially since their price has not stressed me out. I know I couldn't afford them in Italy or the U.S, but here, for instance, I can display a dozen calla lilies for just a little over a dollar. I can even see them from my kitchen as I stow away all the produce I have bought.

The Gourmet Get-Together

A while back, Sandy, Anabel and I had lunch at the Chandelier, long considered one of the best restaurants in San José. As it so often happens, eating delicious food caused the conversation to drift to the topic of other delicious meals.

As we went though our list of favorite foods, I rested my fork in my plate of poached salmon with champagne sauce and confessed.

"I really like a good hot dog," I said. "Especially since my operation, I've been craving them." I cringed, waiting for my companions to reprimand me, as my friends and family have, for even thinking about hot dogs after open-heart surgery. Instead, Sandy put down her fork in the middle of a bite of *corvina amandine*.

"I love hot dogs, too." she said. "And now we can get Hebrew National at PriceSmart."

Anabel looked at the bite of steak she was about to take. "I think I like hot dogs almost as much as I like steak," she confessed.

I had found kindred spirits. We discussed the hot dogs in New York and Coney Island, boiled hot dogs versus grilled hot dogs, and where to find hot dogs that are long enough to fit the bun, and how important freshly chopped tomato and onion are to a hot dog. We agreed it was wonderful that the U.S. Embassy and Residents'

Committee sponsor the Fourth of July picnic with free hot dogs. We debated chili dogs (Sandy is from the South) as opposed to hot dogs with sauerkraut (I'm from the North). Anabel declared she likes them both, but really prefers cheddar cheese and relish on her hot dogs. (She is from Costa Rica.) Then we planned a hot dog dinner as soon as Sandy could get Hebrew Nationals.

The great day came. Sandy invited three other hot dog lovers – Tania, Silvia and Judith. Sandy couldn't get enough Hebrew Nationals (only one and a half per person), so we also had Polish hot dogs from Little Israel. Anabel brought potato salad, Sandy made baked beans and chili, Tania and Silvia brought cucumber and onion salad, Judith brought killer cookies and I brought sauerkraut and a jar of hot fudge sauce.

We dined. We helped ourselves to seconds. Sandy had grilled the hot dogs to perfection. The beans reminded me of Boston. We ate and talked and told jokes. It doesn't get much better than that. And, of course, good food gets a group talking about other great dishes and dinners.

We talked about the great ethnic food newly available and the new restaurants opening in and around San José. I reminded everyone that I had predicted in 1995, perhaps a bit hyperbolically, that Costa Rica would one day become the dining Mecca of the Western World, what with new immigrants and a climate where anything grows.

Then we got on to the subject of our own favorite food (besides hot dogs). In the middle of this discussion I put down my sauerkraut-covered Hebrew National and confessed . . . .

The next time we meet, we may include deviled eggs.

Whatever Happened to La Plume de Ma Tante?

I needed a new pen so I sauntered into Sauter's to check out what they had. Ever since I came to Costa Rica I have had a problem buying pens. *La pluma*, the Spanish word for the French *plume* (which I learned in school) is how I bought a pen when I lived in Majorca. It never gets me the right object in Costa Rica, and by the time I find the Bic or Papermate that I want, I still haven't figured out the word for pen – I just take it to the cashier and silently pay for it. The other two words I knew were *lápiz* and *lapicero*. Maybe here one of those means pen. So when the knowledgeable-looking fellow came up to help me, my first question was "What is the difference between *lápiz* and *lapicero?*"

"Ah," he said, compassionately, taking a number 2 pencil from the rack. "This is a *lapis*" (he spoke pretty good English). Then he pulled an elegant looking pen from another rack and said, "This is *a lapicero.*"

"Don't you have any Papermates?" I asked.

"No," he said. "We only buy Faber Castell from Germany." That didn't make me too happy. But he proceeded to show me the wonderful features of this nice slim 'pen'. You pushed the top as you put your thumb at the mouth of the pen and the nib came out. I tried writing with it – it had a very fine point, which I liked, but it wasn't very dark. Also, the price was 1700 colones, which is not what I wanted to pay for a pen that I would lose in no time. He said he had had his pen for a year and no problems and that I could buy refills very cheaply. "How often do you need refills?" I asked. It depends on whether or not you break the point, I was told. "You mean the point breaks off?" I asked, amazed. Those Germans, what will they come up with next? And why?

It was not until he showed me the eraser in case I made a mistake that it began to dawn on me that a *lapicero* was a mechanical pencil. This conversation had lasted even longer than the one I had in Spain with an Englishman who began the exchange with saying (I thought), "What a pity, they've changed the Rs in Spain." I responded that it was more than a pity; it was ridiculous because communication would come to a standstill. He said that actually Spain would be more readily available to other countries. It wasn't until I allowed that the good news was I always had trouble trilling the Rs anyway, and he asked, "How can one trill the time?" that I realized that he was saying that Spain was going to change its siesta HOURS.

This time I just laughed and said, "Actually I just want something simple like a Bic. What do you call those things?"

"Oh," he said. "We call them *bolígrafos.*" (Accent on second syllable, I mentally noted.) "*Grafos* is from the Greek for writing," he added knowledgeably. "And *boli,* well, *boli* . . .*"

"Is for ball as in ball point," I said. "That is exactly what I want."

Una pluma, I learned, is a pen that you dip in ink, like the old quill pens. Paying for my new pen, I engaged the cashier in a conversation in which I used the word *bolígrafo* three times, because that is supposed to be the charm of learning something new.

Happiness is a New Water Heater

I was astonished the other day when I started to write with my new Farber Castell pen and no ink came out. Then I was indignant. Three weeks and the ink was used up? I decided not to take that lying down and so I went

113

back to Sauter's where I had bought it, confident that the salesman would remember me.

Deciding not to use an indignant approach (indignant gets you nowhere in Costa Rica), I stayed astonished. Inside the store was the tall salesclerk of before, standing by some shelves. I walked over to the pen department and he followed me, asking how he could serve me. I whipped out my pen and asked him if he remembered me, I had bought it about three weeks before, I explained. He didn't remember me. "You taught me the word *bolígrafo*," I said. Then he did remember – as all good teachers remember good students. "I can't believe it," I said, my voice quivering with astonishment. "But this wonderful German pen no longer works. What can I do?"

"No problem," he replied. He plucked it from my hand and walked behind the counter, took out a new pen, tested it, and handed it to me. Then, with a dramatic flourish, he tossed mine into the wastebasket.

"Thank you very much," I said, now *genuinely* astonished.

Walking out of the store, I wondered if he would retrieve the pen to check out my honesty. I felt a bit guilty that he didn't do it immediately. Maybe I just hadn't been using it correctly.

Once home, Dannys, our super, told me they would be coming to put in a new water heater for me. I have been asking for this for only four years, ever since I became convinced that the reason I had no hot water pressure was due to the heater, especially since grass was growing out of it. In the last couple of days, Dannys had installed a new plastic roof over my laundry room, and now it no longer leaks. And the repairman from Samsung had come to fix the knob on my little washing machine so I no longer had to bail water. I was on a roll.

Two men actually showed up the next day, a very good-natured older man and his young assistant. They carried the shiny brand new tank through my kitchen to the laundry and, after the installation, cleaned up the mess they had made. As soon as the heater was installed and the electricity turned back on, I dashed into the bathroom to check the shower. Nothing came out. The installer smiled like a co-conspirator and told me to be patient. He then went into the bathroom and a few minutes later the water was running. He opened the shower and the strongest spray I have seen in six years came out of the showerhead. I could hardly wait for them to leave so I could test it.

I told him that I turned off the electricity to the heater every night to save money. He said that it was wiser to leave the tank on overnight and turn it off during the day. More efficient. His young assistant nodded wisely in agreement. I didn't ask him why. I worked it out for myself that maybe because it was warmer during the day, the water stayed hot. As they were leaving and I was thanking them, the older man said, "Now you won't have to shower like this anymore." And he pushed himself against the door and tilted his head in a very plausible imitation of what I had been going through.

Taking a shower that night I discovered I had plenty of hot water with enough force so I didn't have to sidle up against the wall. I also discovered that, after taking lukewarm showers for so many years, I can't handle a really hot shower anymore. Now I understand how so many Costa Ricans can take cold showers. It is all a matter of adaptation. I went to bed very pleased with the events of the week: ink was coming out of my new pen, hot water was coming out of my shower, the laundry roof no longer leaked, and the water was emptying from my washing machine without my bailing it. Happiness is such a relative thing.

The Joys of Dining at Home Alone

Crowds have been gathering in many places around the world lately. The Summer Olympics in Athens, Greece, have brought together thousands. In New York, several thousand people gathered at Madison Square Garden for the Republican Convention, and tens of thousands more were in the streets to protest. Here in Costa Rica (where everything is on a smaller scale), strikers have been marching and blocking the streets and highways protesting what the government is doing. And, at a lovely ranch in the country, one hundred and fifty people attended a picnic to register voters for the upcoming 2004 U.S. presidential election.

Some of these activities have been televised and many of us have watched all of these people from the solitude of our living rooms, or wherever we have our TVs. I'm talking about those of us who live alone – and we seem to be in the millions. Now I want to get away from the madding crowd to talk about one aspect of living alone. Living alone, one gets to eat alone quite often. Many people find this onerous – some of my friends find eating alone so unappetizing they hardly bother to cook. I have some happy suggestions.

Cooking for yourself may not be fun, but it is an opportunity to try out new recipes that you will want to serve to company. No? How about, eating alone means you can eat whatever you want wherever you want. Standing at the sink is not recommended, but I confess I eat breakfast standing at my counter – I started doing that when I was working. One can get careless with one's manners. Don't let that happen to you. Bad habits are much easier to establish than good habits. At least don't talk to yourself with your mouth full. (Talking to themselves is another thing people living alone tend to do.)

But the best thing about eating alone is what you can eat. And here I will quote writer Fay Maschler in her essay "Sole Food," because she has said it better than I can. "What you must do is serve yourself delicious food that takes practically no preparation and is extravagant enough to buy to make you thankful that it needn't be shared." There you have it – the joy of eating alone.

I happen to love snails, more elegantly known as *escargots*. Once in a great while I order them in restaurants. After carrying them through a dozen moves, I finally left behind my little snail dishes and the prongs with which to eat them. One day I realized I can still eat them without the paraphernalia. A can of twelve snails at the *AutoMercado* is ¢1300. I suggest you serve six at one time – and don't make the mistake of eating the remaining six the following day – it is just too much richness. Which brings me to another cautionary note: eating alone doesn't mean stuffing yourself.

Recipe for six snails: Wash and drain the snails and cut in half. In a small ovenproof casserole, about an inch deep, melt at least 3 tablespoons of butter with 3 cloves of garlic minced, 2 tablespoons of chopped parsley and a dash of brandy, salt and pepper. Add the snails, swishing them around to cover with mixture. Bake at 400 degrees in your toaster oven until the butter bubbles. (You could probably heat them in your microwave.) Enjoy them with some good French bread.

Another food I love is prosciutto ham. This is really expensive: about ¢1800 for just 100 grams cut paper-thin. I can make a meal of melon wrapped in prosciutto. Another joy of eating alone: you can do that with no one saying, "Where's the vegetable?" You can eat veggies at the next meal.

117

My other extravagance is imported Fontina cheese. This is available at Saretto's for about ¢18,000 a kilo. I eat it on toast. Top a slice of toast with thinly sliced tomatoes and then slices of Fontina. Put in the toaster oven till cheese melts.

Those are just a few ideas. I am sure others, with different tastes, have good ideas, too.

Now, you can go back to watching TV. You never turned it off? Oh dear! Another bad habit living alone nurtures.

Thoughts While Making Gnocchi Verdi

One of my favorite dishes is *Gnocchi Verdi*, which is made not with potatoes, but with ricotta cheese and spinach (and thus is low in fats and carbohydrates). The recipe I have calls for a package of frozen chopped spinach, or a pound of fresh. But the spinach here is quite different from U.S. spinach. The leaf is much thicker, and it is sold at the *feria* attached to stalks. In short, it takes time to remove the spinach leaves from the stalks. Rolling the little finished gnocchi into half-inch balls also takes time. So I have time to think.

I thought about the U.S. Congresswoman who said that the prisoners at Guantánamo had gained twenty pounds since being there. She was using this as evidence that they were being well treated. Well, in this day and age of dieting, gaining twenty pounds is not necessarily a sign of good health or good treatment. Under-eating is now considered the secret to a long and healthy life. Also, maybe the prisoners are being fed lots of starches and carbohydrates. They aren't healthy, either. Maybe they have gained weight because they are not getting any exercise. They have nothing to do but eat and sit around all day. What is their cholesterol now?

Then I thought about the American soldier who was a prisoner during the Gulf War. He said that he was fed only one meal a day and lost twenty-three pounds in his fifteen days of captivity. He didn't say if he was overweight when he was captured. How is his cholesterol now? I can just hear some doctors planning the new diet that will replace the South Beach Diet: "The One Meal a Day Diet – lose twenty pounds your first fifteen days."

I was also thinking about the increase in obesity here in Costa Rica. When I visited here in the late 80s, I don't think I saw one really fat person, at least not in San José or the places I visited. Today, I notice them more and more. I have decided that it is not affluence that brings obesity. ("You can't be too rich or too thin," goes the saying.) It is the importation of some of the trappings of the "developed world." Such things as fast-food restaurants, TVs, cars. One can argue that all of these take money. Not necessarily. It may only mean that what money there is, is being spent differently.

Now, before you start thinking I should be ashamed of myself for treating some very serious matters so frivolously, let me say that I am doing what I can not to think any more about the horrors that have been unleashed in that Pandora's Box that is Iraq. It is the elephant in my living room and I am trying not to talk about it. So I am staying in my kitchen cooking and thinking of the absurdities of our times.

My gnocchi turned out just fine with the local spinach. But I had two egg whites left over. I could have just put them in the refrigerator, but no, I had to check out my littlest cook book, *The Good Egg,* which has 200 recipes for leftover whites or yolks. I decided upon divinity fudge. I almost rejected the idea because it called for two and a half cups of sugar. I never cook anything that calls for two and a half cups of sugar! But I pressed on. Well, the

119

sugar, water and corn syrup were merrily boiling when I decided to check out divinity in my old, old *Joy of Cooking*. The first bit of advice was "Pick a dry day." I looked out the open door to my balcony. The rain had stopped but the thunder was threatening more. This is the rainy season. Taking a lesson from George Bush, I stayed the course. I beat the egg whites and when the syrup was ready, slowly poured it into the whites as I kept beating. Soon I realized that it was ballooning much too much for the bowl and I had to transfer it to a larger bowl. That's when I thought I had invented a new recipe for super glue. The white foam was sticking to everything.

When I thought it was ready, I dropped it in spoonfuls onto waxed paper. We used to make sea foam fudge, which is a variation of divinity. But when we dropped the lumps on waxed paper they stayed in nice little lumps. These spread out into flat coins. A little voice kept saying, "Cut and run, Jo." But I stayed the course and got out more wax paper for a few more. The recipe is supposed to make fifty pieces. That's when I checked what more the Rombauers had to say. It was, "This candy does not keep well." Great, fifty pieces and they don't keep well. I decided to walk away from the problem for a bit, hoping the candy would firm up.

When I checked them again, my large white coins looked like they had jimmies on them. I put on my glasses and discovered they were swarming with little black ants. Some weren't swarming, they were stuck. Talk about insurgents! Where do these ants come from so suddenly? That decided it. The "candies" went into the trash and the bowl of the remaining mixture into the sink under running water. I still had an incredible mess to clean up. Next time, I will just beat those two egg whites and have a low-fat, low-carbohydrate omelet.

Politics Here and There

The Cruelty of Countries

Our conversation began while Sandy, Anabel and I were having lunch. Anabel read out loud an editorial in *La Nación* (our leading newspaper) by Oscar Arias, Costa Rica's Nobel Laureate for Peace. In it, he says that terrorism is not the only threat to a country; there are the threats of illiteracy, environmental degradation and hunger that must be addressed. We talked about the unbelievable suffering that people endure, and Sandy mentioned a movie about the holocaust and how her husband couldn't bear to watch it. Then we began talking about the different people of the world who have faced terrible adversity with bravery and courage, even stoicism. As we mentioned different people, Anabel said, rather sadly, that Costa Ricans did not have the stamina, the solidarity nor the strength to withstand disaster, to undergo really hard times. There is a saying in Costa Rica that a disaster or scandal will last only fifteen days, and after that it is forgotten.

As we talked about the Jews during the reign of Hitler, Russia under Stalin, repression in China, the suffering of South African Blacks during apartheid, Ethiopia, Uganda and other countries of Africa, the Chileans when Pinochet was in power, Iraq under Saddam Hussein, Argentineans during the time of the Disappeared, I began to realize something.

Indeed, "War is hell," as General Sherman said, but the truly prolonged suffering of different peoples has been caused as much by the cruel leadership of their own government as it has been by war. In all of the groups we brought up, it was the leaders of their own countries who had caused their misery. We went on to add El Salvador and countries that engaged in civil war, such as Nicaragua, Spain and the United States, and of despotic regimes such as Guatemala. The list was mind-boggling. Talking about the other countries of Central America, I found an answer to comfort Anabel.

The governments of Costa Rica have not been less corrupt financially than other countries, but this country's leaders, for the most part, have not combined institutionalized cruelty with corruption. The people of Costa Rica have not had a history of oppression and suffering. Spain neglected this mountainous little possession that had no gold. When Spain withdrew its colonial rule over Central America, Costa Ricans were simply notified that they were free.

This is not to say that there has never been suffering and war here. The poor of all societies have always suffered. A civil war erupted in Costa Rica in 1948, when compromise among the different factions proved impossible. This war was as bloody and vicious as any civil war. The difference was its brevity. President Picado had no stomach for this fighting because among the young rebels were former students and sons of friends. It started March 10, 1948, and on April 13, peace negotiations began.

Given their history it is doubtful that Ticos will ever be called upon to prove their mettle through political suffering. In fact, a recent survey has shown that the majority of Ticos are quite content with their lot. (It must be said that their lot includes almost perfect weather and gorgeous scenery, two things money can't buy.)

Now this realization on my part that there are cruel regimes does not mean that I favor war to end them. War, to my mind is never a solution, and besides, some leaders start wars just to take peoples' minds off their suffering. Fortunately, that is not something Costa Ricans have to face.

(Note: my thanks to the family Biesanz for *The Ticos: Culture and Society in Costa Rica (1999)*, a good English-language source for the history of the country.)

Election Day in the Civilized "Developing World"

As I write this, today, Sunday, Feb.3, 2002, it is Election Day in Costa Rica. It is always on Sunday so that everyone can vote, and since people must vote in their own province, it is also a reunion day for families and old friends. To make it all even easier, free transportation is offered by the various parties so that people can go home. To insure clear-headed voting, liquor is not sold from Friday night until Monday morning. Obviously, Costa Rica really wants its citizens to vote.

I am watching TV only periodically this Sunday, mainly to get glimpses of the different provinces around the country. The weather is beautiful everywhere. I decide to walk downtown during the last hour of voting, while it is still light. On my way, I ask some men sitting on the front steps of a house if they know who is winning. No, they say, they won't know until 9 p.m. tonight. There will be no winner announced until all the provinces are heard from.

There are something like 13 candidates representing every party and philosophy you can imagine, from Libertarian to Communist. According to my neighbor, Darrylle, there is even one candidate who is running on a platform of change, just change, with the philosophy that anything is better than what they have now.

The three main candidates are Abel Pacheco, Rolando Araya and Otón Solís. The only one I have met is Señor Solís, who left the *Partido Liberación Nacional* and is now heading a new party, the *Partido Accion Ciudadana*. He is running on an anti-corruption platform (in fact,

125

everyone is running on an anti-corruption platform, to some extent). I heard him speak at a luncheon I attended some months ago. He was eloquent and idealistic. He has a Ph.D. in economics. He said that if corruption is not stopped, the people of Costa Rica are going to vote in a dictator. Many of us were impressed, and I even thought that he might have a chance.

On my way downtown I walk past the three justice buildings and notice how clean the streets are. They are spotless, swept clean even before the new broom has been elected. I notice the cleanliness and the noise. The noise is coming from the cars, sometimes a lone car, sometimes caravans, displaying the different flags representing their parties and honking their horns. The flags they can use every year, unlike placards and leaflets.

I decide to go via the new esplanade between the National Park and the courts. It is most pleasant — another three or four blocks for pedestrians only. The houses and other buildings along the way all look newly painted, and for some reason the district makes me think of England. Once again on a trafficked street, the cars and flags and horns are celebrating. Everybody is waving at everybody else. Some are displaying their ink-stained hands showing they have already voted.

There seem to be a lot of yellow and orange flags so I ask two young women, also on their way to town, which party they represent. (I really already knew; I just want to start a conversation.) They tell me it is the party of Otón Solís. "There are a lot of them," I remark. "Yes," they smile. "Maybe we'll win."

Once downtown I find a table at the News Café (and wonder if I am going to make this my hangout). I am sitting on the low balcony that juts out onto Avenida Central, the pedestrian mall, and is the closest thing to a sidewalk café I can find. It is quite pleasant sitting there with my notebook.

It has been years since I have written anything in a sidewalk café. I decide I'll have a cappuccino, but nobody comes to take my order. Finally, I call a waiter over and ask him the names of the three principal parties. He doesn't know. I show him I am shocked. He smiles and placates me by saying he is not Tico, he is Colombian, and he goes off to ask another waiter. I get the information, but forget to ask for a cappuccino, and no one else comes to take my order.

I stay downtown until after dark, then find the beautiful breezy day has turned quite chilly, the breeze now a wind with an icy edge. I walk to three different corners, even the corner across from the Del Rey Hotel. There are always taxis there. But there are few now, and those few prefer to take the gringos and their new young acquaintances.

Finally I am on Second Avenue and have just seen my bus leave. I wave a taxi just as three young men do. The *taxista* signals them he is picking me up. I apologize to them and thank him profusely.

As we ride along I ask him who has won the election. He says Pacheco is in the lead, but there will have to be a runoff. "In Costa Rica," he says, "we don't lean toward the left or the right; we go down the middle. We don't have an army, we don't fight wars; instead we plant beans and rice and live in peace." It sounds good to me.

When I get home, I turn on the TV. Pacheco, the most grandfatherly of the three front runners (who is also a psychiatrist) is speaking, explaining to his cheering supporters that there will be a runoff because he won just under 39 percent of the vote, and the law says the winner must garner at least 40 percent. Otón Solís got 26 percent. Pacheco urges his followers to go out and vote when the time comes. Once over 90 percent of the voting population voted. In recent years the number has been dropping.

In answer to some question I don't hear, he says, "*Costarricenses hacen todo con gusto.*" ("Costa Ricans do everything willingly and with pleasure" is my translation.) Yes, you do, I think, and you do it with considerable grace and good sense too.

I turn off the TV and have a thought I often have: the best thing Costa Rica has to offer the world is its own example.

I'll Take the Potholes

Among primates, so the belief goes, it is a strategy of older males to send the younger ones off to fight so that they can get the females and then, in proper evolutionary spirit, pass along their genes. Costa Rica has managed to short-circuit this evolutionary ploy.

On Monday, December 1, Costa Rica celebrated the 55th anniversary of the abolishment of its army. Perhaps I should say armies. In 1948, after a six-week civil war, José "Pepe" Figueres was head of the winning faction, and therefore declared President. But he was left with two armies, one of them part of the faction which had opposed him. Not wanting a coup, he made a decision worthy of Solomon. He abolished the institution of the military altogether (and in another brilliant move, gave women the vote).

President Bush has said more than once that democratic countries do not go to war with one another. Costa Rica has done him one better: it has not gone to war with ANYONE since 1948. I attended the celebration on the 50th anniversary five years ago. It was held in the Plaza de la Democracia in front of the National Museum, a bullet-pocked building that was once a fortress. On the 50th anniversary there were a couple of ex-presidents present, and the ceremony ended with the release of dozens of butterflies. I had to laugh: butterflies instead of Air Force jets screaming overhead to show the country's strength.

This year the celebration was held inside the museum because it was raining. First Vice President Lineth Saborio was there in person, but most of the speeches by a number of important people (I recognized only former President Arias), were on a screen. It was still inspiring. When the military was first abolished, a large portion of the money that would have gone into preparing for war was invested in schools, hospitals, clinics and universities. In a short time Costa Rica surpassed its neighbors in education, and medical and social services.

The benefits of not having a military are practically endless. Without a military we have no young men who have been maimed, both physically and mentally, by the experience of war. No body bags and funerals for young people who were in the prime of life. No disabled veterans struggling to make a life, or living homeless on the streets. No families separated and broken by a member going off to war. No children left orphans, or worse, killed or crippled by bombs and weapons, or themselves carrying weapons and learning to kill before they have learned to read. This part of the earth is not being polluted by the waste products of nuclear, biological and chemical weapons. (We humans make enough waste without adding even more non-biodegradable poisons.)

And think of all the money that is saved by not having to rebuild buildings and infrastructure that are senselessly demolished. And then there are the illnesses we avoid from contaminated water, along with the famine that so often comes with war. Among the other casualties we avoid creating are the refugees who flee their countries and way of life in order to survive. Instead, Costa Rica has become a refuge for people fleeing from other countries, like Nicaragua and Colombia. Refugees outnumber every other kind of traveler.

There are some downsides to no army. I became aware of one when I visited Nicaragua a few years ago. It soon became apparent that the roads, and especially the highways, in Nicaragua were in much better condition than those in Costa Rica. When I commented on this I was told that the roads were well-built, thanks to help from the U.S., so that tanks could travel on them more easily. If that is the trade-off, I'll take the potholes.

How to Achieve a Critical Mass

The other day I was thinking about an article about critical mass I read some time ago in the *New Yorker*. Critical mass is the minimum volume or number it takes for something to happen or a change to take place. Think of it as the straw that breaks the camel's back. It came to mind, as I pondered the news that the pollution in the city is getting worse. Since San José does not have heavy industry spewing black smoke, the cause for this pollution seems obvious – the increase in the number of vehicles and the amount of ugly fumes they exude.

For years the lovely breeze that blows in the Central Valley has been enough to keep everything under control. It used to be that only a few cars were parked on the street leading to my street. Now they are bumper to bumper and even squeezed in on the corners. There are two parking attendants on the street. (A Tica friend told me that these self-employed car-watchers used to have shoe shine stands but, with the increase in cars, there were fewer requests for their services.) Downtown it is not unusual for a car to wait through three changes of a traffic light before it can proceed. At dawn I can see a rim of smog on the once blue horizon. A critical mass has been reached and the breeze can no longer blow the pollution away.

I try to think how I, as a pedestrian, can help alleviate this problem. Except for throwing wrappers and cigarette butts on the sidewalk – and yes, I must admit, there are a few spitters – pedestrians don't pollute much. Smoking on the streets has become more popular as it becomes the only place a person can safely smoke and get only dirty looks. But generally, our huffing and puffing doesn't begin to compare with auto pollution.

So what about buses? Buses pollute, but not as much per person as a car with only the driver. Buses are as quick a way as any to get through town, and one can read while doing it. A lot of the buses in the city are bought second-hand from another country. Often they are former school buses with tiny plastic seats that encourage dieting.

The other day I boarded one of these buses. Climbing aboard, I was immediately aware of a difference and when I sat down, tears nearly came to my eyes. It was not the same old bus with hard, rickety narrow seats. It was new. The seats were cushioned, with high backs, and were ample enough for an adult to be comfortable. I smiled with pleasure. I felt special and cared about. All of this for me? Just to go across town?

I remembered my days at the International House in San Jose, California, where one of my goals was to give the residents – students from around the world – a home as clean, comfortable and luxurious as we could on our budget. The motivations were 1) I wanted the students to feel special and cared about, and 2) if they felt like that, they would want to be where they were and take good care of their surroundings.

It worked at the I-House and it was working here with me on this bus. I wanted to take good care of the bus so that I could enjoy it as long as possible. I was already looking forward to riding the bus again, and I hadn't even disembarked! I felt special warmth towards the city for treating me so well.

Lately I have noticed that there are more nice buses on the streets. That is when I again thought about critical mass. The snarl of traffic of one-passenger cars continues to get worse. If more and more buses are replaced with inviting beauties, and the city carries on a heavy-duty "ride the bus" and "walking is good exercise" campaign, maybe the scales will tip and the people sitting in their cars will notice and start riding the bus and walking more. I am waiting for gridlock and pollution to get so bad for so many people and city officials that something gets done.

Once all of this has been accomplished, I'll work on achieving a critical mass of protesters to get them to put one more step on the buses so those of us who are getting older and shorter can climb on the bus in the first place.

People Power

Usually I am happy to write about the pleasures and occasional frustrations of living in Costa Rica. But recently it has been difficult to dwell on these subjects when I am so aware of what is going on in the rest of the world.

Hardly a day goes by that I am not grateful to be here, where I don't have to be thinking about a possible terrorist attack or a falling bomb. Not that Costa Rica is without violence or crime; it has its share. But it is still a country committed to peace, and so peace is what we will get. It is the sabre-rattling of countries committed to war as a means to peace that has me worried.

A friend in the U.S. forwarded a letter from Israel. It was about a recent demonstration by people who are also committed to peaceful means of creating co-existence between the Palestinians and the Jews who live there.

According to this letter, over 10,000 Jews and Arabs gathered in the Museum Plaza in Tel Aviv to speak out for peace and to support the growing number of Israeli soldiers who are refusing to "serve an army that kills children."

Reading the letter made me remember 12 years ago when I was taking my dream trip, a train ride from Athens, Greece, to Oslo, Norway. I was leaving Norway after visiting my friend Nina, and she had come to the train station to see me off – I was now on my way to England. While we were sitting in my assigned compartment making the small talk people make when they must part, we both noticed a youngish man on the platform saying goodbye to friends. We noticed him because he was wearing a pale blue polyester bell-bottomed suit. We looked at each other with raised eyebrows and smirks. Who, in 1990, would wear such a suit?

As it turned out, of course, his seat was in my compartment, right next to me. After the train left the station we had a conversation, which is what you do on trains. He was a botanist or biologist (it has been 12 years, and I have forgotten details) and a college professor from the Czech Republic.

For years, he said, he had annually applied for permission to go to Norway to study at a special institute, and for years his government had refused, even though Norway had a grant waiting for him. Then in November of 1989, something unbelievable happened. It started when people were gathered in Prague to celebrate something like the end of the Nazi occupation. At one point, their own police fired into the crowd of celebrants to disperse them. The soldiers who fired upon them were so young they would not have remembered World War II. This was, he said, the final straw of the oppression they had lived under since the end of that war.

The celebration turned into a demonstration against the government, and the next day tens of thousands more showed up in the square to protest quietly, and the day after that, even more. He said that he lived outside the city, but arrived on Monday to go to the University and joined what was now over a million people, "who were like one organism, with one mind" protesting their government's policies, demanding free elections.

In a matter of days, the Communist Party leadership resigned, and the rest, as they say, is history. The young scientist's request was finally granted, and he put on the only suit he had and traveled outside his country for the first time in his life. Now he was on his way home after the most exciting six months of his life.

Years later, I remember that young man at whom I had snickered and who told me a story with a lesson I would never forget. People power does exist and change can be brought about peacefully . . . _and_ you never know who your teachers are going to be.

And Not a Drop to Drink Pretty Soon

Last week I was off to Arenal with my friend Sandy and her friend Jenny, who was visiting from Australia. We traveled by car and Jenny, who has visited many developing countries, noted how clean Costa Rica was. That made me take notice, because when I first moved here I would not have said that, but looking at the roadside all along the way and the small towns we went through, I saw that she was right. There was almost no litter. The campaign must be working.

It rained most of the time we were in Fortuna. It rains a lot in that part of Costa Rica. Speaking of rain, I also noted that the water tasted much better than the water I drink in San José. All of this made me think about the talk I had heard at a luncheon. Maureen Ballesteros, Central American chair of the Global Water Partnership, and Maria Elena Fournier, president of the CR environmental group YISKI, talked about water and environmental pollution.

We got a lot of statistics beginning with the fact that 70% of the earth is water, and 95% of that is salt water. And finally, only 2.5 percent of what's left is available for human use. The next world crisis (to my mind) is going to be a water shortage. Given the continued overuse, pollution, and climate changes that are making for longer hotter summers and shorter wetter winters, the 2.2 million people who die every year from water-borne diseases is going to triple and the number of people who don't have access to water (now over 1 billion) is going to get bigger. The prediction was that by 2025 the demand for water will grow by 17% and 2/3 of the world's population will have problems.

I, of course, was very interested in the situation in Costa Rica. Overall, as we all know, Costa Rica has plenty of rain. The Pacific coast, however, gets only 30% of the water and faces shortages. Cutting down forests to make way for cattle grazing has been partly responsible in the northern area. According to the statistics I heard, in Costa Rica there are 31,318 cubic meters of water per person available as compared to 400 cubic meters per person in Spain. Not all of that water is potable. Costa Ricans use an average of 187 liters a day.

Ground water is the principal source of the water we use and the Central Valley sits on lots of it, but much of it is contaminated by both individual and industrial use. Mismanagement and neglect further cripple the availability of potable water. There are still many people in Costa Rica who have no access to municipal water and, as I write this, I am sure somewhere in Costa Rica people have just had their water turned off. The water delivery system has not been updated since the 1980s. At the moment, neither the government nor the people seem to want to take steps to correct matters – except on the part of some to fight privatization of the distribution of water.

It would cost about $925 million to modernize the water delivery systems here. That seems a pittance when you think about the money the U.S. is pouring into Iraq; to Costa Rica, however, that is a lot of money. But what a worthwhile investment! Eventually, Costa Rica could export pure water to the thirsty rest of the world. And it is a renewable resource.

However, the road (or should I say river?) to selling water is fraught with countless problems and pitfalls, including the cobbler's children syndrome, so perhaps we should start small and just try to conserve water and not add to its pollution.

Maybe if we start at home, industries will follow and not dump pollutants into our rivers. Two suggestions made at the luncheon were to use washing soda to wash clothes instead of harmful detergents. (I am told washing soda is available at pharmacies very cheap.) And instead of using all those harmful cleaning liquids, try vinegar and water. I am thinking about the litter-free countryside we saw on our trip. A public education campaign to conserve and preserve clean water would probably work, too.

Gail's Kids Now Have a Chance for a Future

There is a popular saying that begins, "The greatness of a country is measured by how it treats ___ " . . . then you can fill in the blank with the group of the moment: "its children," "its sick," "its old people." Almost any group is used except "its millionaire CEOs." One of the sad realities of Costa Rica, and especially San José, is the number of children who have had to make their home on the streets. Most are there because they come from grinding poverty or dysfunctional, abusive families. (Usually these two conditions go together.)

Most of the kids living on the streets are drug users, usually glue, which helps them get through the days of boredom and the long nights of hunger and cold and the lack of any of the necessities that most of us take for granted. It is encouraging that President Pacheco is taking note of their condition. Fortunately, for some of them, they have a friend.

Sunday I was at a fund-raising brunch for these children – or rather for the children who have been rescued by Gail Nystrom. Gail is the founder and hands-on Director of the *Fundación Humanitaria Costarricense*. Thirteen of the 15 young people who have found a home thanks to Gail were at the fund-raiser. They call her *"la gringa loca."* *Gringos* call her the "Saint of San José." What she has taken on does require the vision and heart of a Mother Teresa, but instead of easing people to their deaths, Gail is leading these youths to a new life.

When Gail talks about how scared she was when she picked up the first children, I remember with painful shame the night I was coming home in a taxi and saw a child who couldn't have been more than five, sleeping in a doorway. I hesitated and asked the cab driver to slow down. But what went through my mind next was, "What do I do with him tomorrow? What if he is full of lice or worse? What if he wakes up and bops me one and robs me?" The voice inside me that said, "He is only 5 years old, for heaven sake," did not get heard over my fears. So, we drove on.

Gail didn't drive on, and she had just as many fears as I. The kids she picked up were in their teens. They were like feral animals, distrustful and fearful, without adult friends, certainly not the police.

The early months were not easy. They smashed things, they were rebellious, they challenged Gail at every turn, daring and expecting her to throw them out. Instead, she gave them more love and worked harder with them.

These were the teenagers at the brunch, and they were pretty impressive, social and gracious in dealing with grownups. Their art, their candles and the little grasshoppers they had made from grass, were on display. I bought a drawing done by 18-year-old Daniel. I really like it and expect one day he will be a well-known artist.

Sixteen-year-old Marianela told us about her life. When she talked about living on the streets, she had to keep remembering not to hang her head. Then, beginning with a radiant smile, she talked about her life today. These kids look after their home, do their own cooking, take classes (some are even learning English) and are planning for the future. Other young people are serving as interns with Gail. These young people are from other countries, often recent college graduates who haven't yet decided what they want to do with their lives. I am sure this experience will affect their decisions.

Women on the March

Last Friday I was in the Cleveland Store (a *ropa Americana*), and I saw a T-shirt that said: "Take Back the Night." It reminded me of all the women who have marched in protest against the dangers they face when they venture out at night. The T-shirt was far too large for me. The woman who wore that, I thought, at least could defend herself. The most help women have heard over the years is the advice not to go out alone at night.

Years ago I was on a task force organized to solve the problem of street prostitution in downtown San José, California. There were a number of suggested solutions, all aimed at greater punishment for the prostitutes, such as harassing them when they appeared on the street, giving them longer jail sentences, or simply shipping them out of town.

Finally I suggested that, instead of harassing the supply, we should go after the demand and harass any man who was on the street without a woman. Without a market, the prostitutes would go away, I said, and I pointed out that this would also reduce the attacks on women who were out at night alone. I expected kudos from the other task force members, most of whom were men, for my free-market capitalistic solution. Instead, my idea was greeted with derisive laughter and indignation at the very idea of restricting men's freedom of movement.

Leaving the Cleveland store, I walked to Avenida 2. There was a march getting organized. Costa Rican women were protesting the violence against them, mostly domestic violence. Homemade signs said, "The women of Costa Rica wish to live without violence." A contingency of women from Golfito carried a sign that said, "To live without violence is a right." Two women carried a sign saying, "Lesbians against Violence."

There was a group of school children, another of policewomen. There were old women and young. Most of the women looked poor, but not all. Their faces had something in common, a personal knowledge of what they were protesting, I thought. I had to fight back the tears when I thought of what they all had been through to be here.

When I saw one woman dragging a roughly made cross, I began foraging for my hanky. She was also carrying a very heavy looking backpack. Actually, seeing that backpack saved me from tears because my first and rather irreverent thought was of Ginger Rogers dancing backwards in high heels. Still, I wondered how much good

139

this march would do? Are women any safer on the street at night in the United States? Maybe they never will be, but in the U.S. there are many more shelters for abused women than there used to be and the laws have become more favorable. At the moment there are only two shelters for abused women in all of Costa Rica, but slowly the laws are changing, and with each march, women will gain courage from one another.

I don't know what the woman with the cross intended her message to be, but the message I got was that women have not been given just a cross to bear, but a backpack to boot. Fortunately, we have the strength and endurance to carry both.

Staying Healthy in Costa Rica

Starting the New Year Hitting the Ground Running

A promo on TV for the movie *Con Air* is offering a prize for the most scary flight story. I am thinking of submitting mine.

Mavis and I had just arrived at Bill's house for a luncheon party. Blas, Mavis' driver, helped her out of the car which he had to park on a rather steep incline. I knew he would come and help me, but I figured I could manage, even in sandals and with the six-pack of beer Mavis had in the back seat. So out I stepped. The weight of the six-pack in my left hand and on the downside of the hill was enough to throw me off balance. Not wanting to fall, I stepped in that direction hoping to right myself. Instead, I began to move downhill. Soon (going from zero to 15 mph in ten seconds, I'm sure) I was racing down the hill, beer cans and even my shoes flying in my wake.

Time moved in slow motion and many thoughts crossed my mind: I wished someone were filming this, it had to be hilarious, me in my elegant silk chartreuse slacks, out of control, barreling down the hill in my stocking feet. If this were a movie, I would wind up covered with fake blood, with a wound that would be healed by the next scene. I was also desperately looking for the road to level off so I could slow down. It didn't. Finally, no longer able to keep up with my legs, I took to the air – for about two seconds – and then I made a four point landing (hands, chest, and nose) and, using my toes as brakes, finally slid to a stop.

They are right: taking off and landing are the most dangerous (and painful) parts of flying. Blas, who was running behind me trying to catch up, got to me and lifted me, bleeding real blood and hurting all over. Later he told

143

me the first thing I said was, "The beer, the beer!" The cans were strewn along the road spraying their foaming liquid.

With great presence of mind and concern, he got me into the house and carefully washed my hands and toes. Someone called the Red Cross and the ambulance arrived in just ten minutes. It was decided that my left hand needed stitches and the rest of me more sanitizing, so off we went to the hospital. I was closer to CIMA but, with only *Caja* insurance, I said I wanted to go to Calderón Guardia. We sped along the *autopista* and bounced across town, where thankfully, there was little traffic, its being New Year's Day. When we arrived at Calderón Guardia they took me in by wheelchair. I knew there was no way I could walk. It felt as if I had broken at least four ribs and my left wrist.

When I asked the Red Cross attendants how much the ride was, they said, "Nothing." I shall certainly in the future give generously whenever I see a Red Cross person with his little white and red box. I hope some of my donations will go towards new shock absorbers for their ambulances.

It was one o'clock and I was surprised to see so few people in the hallways. Six hours later, when I left, after several scrubbings, two x-rays (not a single broken bone), an electrocardiogram, three stitches, three shots and two prescriptions, the hospital waiting rooms resembled an airport when all planes have been cancelled. My heart went out to all of those with cuts and bruises worse than mine (I shared their pain), who were still waiting, and to the overworked, yet still compassionate hospital staff who had hours to go.

After one night of going it on my own, I accepted Mavis' offer to stay with her while I recuperated. On the second day of my stay she received a letter from a friend of hers who was getting along in years. She read some of it to me. It said, "Now that I am older, my ears are better for listening and learning; I live one day at a time; and if something which needs doing is risky, I don't do it."

Sounds like good advice.

One Tough Cookie

I used to be inspired by the statement, which I think was a contribution from Ralph Waldo Emerson: "Do the thing and you have the power" . . . to do it again. Now I am a bit cynical and think it only applies from one day to the next and then, only if nothing disastrous has happened.

Yesterday I went downtown to pay bills and get done so many things I have neglected. I haven't done much walking lately and need the exercise. I used to love walking, not only in the city, but even the twenty blocks to the center of the city. Now the journey is fraught with danger. There are the ubiquitous potholes and uneven streets, the huge gutters to be jumped to reach the sidewalks, the buses that come careening around a corner. Downtown is filled with animate and inanimate threats to my equilibrium. I am not the same person I was before I fell.

I was thinking about my brother, who sailed his Chinese junk in the Caribbean for nearly ten years. It was docked in Jacksonville, Florida, one wintry night when his little stove ran out of gas. He decided he had to get another tank or freeze. Once on deck he planned to jump to the dock, but his boat was covered with a thin layer of ice and he slipped, falling into the water, hitting his shoulder on the way down. The fall broke his shoulder and he was having trouble treading water, much less getting out of it. But he realized he would die if he didn't, so with superhuman strength he pulled himself up on the boat and managed to radio for help. When I saw him a couple of years later, he was not the same man I had known. He seemed tentative and cautious. The experience had reshaped him. And now the same thing was happening to me.

I began to wonder if Mike's problem was thinking too much about his close call and not enough about his heroic and successful effort to save himself. I have also been thinking about a realization I came to after hearing of Mama Cass' death from choking on some food. Very often our passions or habits are responsible for our own downfalls. In my case, my love of pretty but not very practical shoes probably had a lot to do with my fall. (Now I would happily wear a pair of modified snowshoes if I could find them.) Yet I had survived WITHOUT A SINGLE BROKEN BONE. I shouldn't feel vulnerable. I am, in fact, one tough cookie.

Yesterday I went downtown. I managed to walk the five blocks to the bus stop and to stand most of the hour it took to pay for my health insurance. Although I took a bus to RACSA, I walked the seven blocks back to the bus stop carrying a bag of groceries. A lot of it was with great effort, and once I even sat down to rest on the steps of the Omni building. I tried to look as if I was just waiting for someone, instead of drop-dead exhausted. I caught a bus to my post office, got my mail and from there hailed a taxi for home, a place I desperately wanted to be.

I gratefully plopped myself down on my beloved sofa, where I could finally think about what I had accomplished. Wow, I thought. You did the thing. While I was congratulating myself, my electric bill was slipped under the door and I realized I would have to do it again tomorrow. I probably could.

With surprising energy and high spirits, I got off the sofa to make my lunch from the delicious things I had bought at the market. That is when I realized I had left my bag of groceries in the taxi – along with my mail, which I had put in the bag. Given the crumbling of conscience in this day and age, I knew I could not expect to see either again.

As my substitute soup was cooking, I pondered how I was going to work on my wits and not despair that I was losing my mind as I was regaining my body.

A Patient's Dilemma

This past week was a musical one ending with the concert at the Teatro Nacional on Sunday at 10:30 a.m. Friend Jerry had an extra ticket for a seat in a *palco principal*, so I was spared the climb to the *galeria lateral*, which I consider to be a dry run for climbers of Mt. Everest. (There are seven different ticket levels at the theater.)

The program was stunning, but then every program our orchestra does is stunning. It was my first opportunity to see our new conductor, Dr. Chosei Komatsu, in action. He is young, charming, and (according to my stereotyping) quite exuberant for a Japanese.

I am a fidget. I think there must be some rule in all books on etiquette that, if you are over five, you remain perfectly still during any musical presentation, especially a symphony. I can't. I fidget. Jerry, next to me, never moved a muscle, not even throughout the last symphony, which lasted forty-five minutes non-stop. His stillness made every move I made more maddening, even to me. A nose that never itches, began to. I clasped and unclasped my hands. I wiggled my toes. My eyes darted around, as I tried to hold my head still, searching for other fidgets. I saw only one. As yet there is no Fidgets Anonymous.

Meanwhile, I was wrong that music and water keep you healthy. I am wrong so much lately, it no longer bothers me. Very early Tuesday morning, I awoke, knowing from the redness of my right arm that I was in for another bout of cellulitis. I hauled myself off to Calderón Guardia's new emergency hospital. It was not an especially happy experience. After waiting an hour, I explained to the young doctor what my problem was and that I needed antibiotics. Before he would concur with my diagnosis he decided we needed to take some tests – x-ray, electrocardiogram, a urine and blood test. Unfortunately, I had to wait three hours before I could get an x-ray. Other doctors had told me that I should get antibiotics immediately, so I was getting more and more worried. But I did all that was necessary.

As I sat waiting to see the doctor again, I remembered many years ago in New York, where I had acquired sinus troubles. I was insured by HIP, which normally provided good health service. In response to a new sinus infection, I made an appointment to get it taken care of. When I called, they asked me if I would become the patient of a new doctor who had just joined, since he was looking for patients. I said yes. The doctor was young and seemed to be trying to acquire the proper doctorly attitude. When I told him that I had a sinus infection, he smiled paternally and said, "Well, shall we let me be the doctor? I think we should take some tests just to make sure that is the problem." I went away with no treatment but more appointments for blood and urine tests. On my next visit I was informed that the tests hadn't come through. I was in pain and as I sat on the examining table tears filled my eyes.

"Look at you," he said. "I think you may be depressed. Perhaps we should make an appointment with a psychologist."

"I *am* depressed," I said. "But it's because I have a very painful sinus infection and nothing is being done about it. I don't need a psychologist for that."

By the end of the week the tests had come back and my thoroughgoing doctor said, "Mrs. Stuart I want to congratulate – oh, it's Miss Stuart, isn't it? Well, I don't think congratulations are in order, but you are pregnant."

After a few seconds of silent incredulity I said, "Doctor, there is no way I can be pregnant. I have a sinus infection." As I slid off the examining table, I added, "I suggest you find a patient with morning sickness who thinks SHE has a sinus infection." And I walked out.

My office companions thought that very funny, but insisted I call the Director of HIP and complain. He immediately made an appointment for me with an ear, nose and throat specialist. After a very short examination the specialist said, "My god, woman, you have the worst sinus infection I've seen in years. Why didn't you come in sooner?"

I sat on his examining table wringing my hands and twisting my feet.

"You'll do something about it right away?" I asked.

"Of course," he said. Then he added, "I notice you tend to fidget quite a bit. I have a daughter like that. She's only five. She'll probably grow out of it."

"Don't count on it," I said.

Remembering all of this at the Calderón Guardia, I gathered my possessions and left before seeing the doctor again. I caught a taxi to the Clínica Duran where, after just two tests (and three more hours), the doctor prescribed antibiotics.

"What did the tests show?" I asked.

"You have an infection – cellulitis," he said.

Favor de Cuidar Mi Campo in this Endless Line

Bureaucratic procedures, also known as red tape and called *trámites* in Spanish, are the bane of my happy life in Costa Rica. The main reason I have a terrible and traumatic time with *trámites* is that I don't know the routines and nobody explains them until after the fact. This is worse than not knowing the steps in a group tap-dancing routine. When you don't know what you are supposed to do here, it usually results in standing in yet another line (or going back to the line you were in before).

All of this is a preface to my visit to the Clínica Duran Monday morning. My appointment was for 7 a.m. I arrived at 6:45, thinking I would be the first in line. I wasn't. I couldn't believe so many Ticos were up and about so early and I was much relieved that I didn't have to join the line waiting in front of the laboratory window. There must have been fifty people in it.

First I waited in line to confirm my appointment with the receptionist, who told me to wait to be called. Then I was called by the preliminary nurse so she could take my blood pressure (a little high) and my weight (ditto). Then I was told to wait to be called. I decided not to try to read because one time when they called my name I didn't hear it and left in a snit after waiting hours without seeing a doctor. It is difficult to tell who is a doctor and who is not. This morning I noted that women doctors wear sexy shoes (as well as stethoscopes) rather than the practical white low-heeled shoes that most nurses wear. I found myself annoyed because I had to stand and a six year old boy sat cross legged on a bench, happily eating one piece of fruit after another. My scowls at his mother were ineffective.

I also noted that there were five women to every man in the waiting room. Later, in another waiting room, I realized the former distribution was because I was in the area for gynecology, family practice and psychiatry.

I got to see the doctor within an hour and he gave me papers ordering a sonogram, mammography and some pills. First I went up to the *farmacia* to leave my order for the pills because that always takes an hour. I was told I had to take my request back downstairs and have the receptionist put my name label on it. I did that, waiting for seven people in front of me, then went back upstairs. Then I went to the main desk to make the appointment for the sonogram. I knew I had to go to Calderón Guardia for my mammogram.

I was told I had to go back to the receptionist to get a label on my referral. This time the line was fourteen people long. I should state right here that I have bad luck with lines. I am the person who, if I choose the shortest-looking line in the market, the checker is new and learning, or the cash register tape runs out just as I get to the counter. In any other line, the person in front of me is holding a place for another person. The woman behind me is holding a baby, so I let her go ahead, and the old guy behind her has a cane and is called to the window before me. And when I finally get to the window, a friend of the receptionist comes up and they chat a bit and then she is quietly (but I notice it) tended to in front of me. All of these things happened as I waited in line this time. In spite of that, by 10:30 I was on my way with my prescription. The good news is that everything was free – well, after paying the monthly insurance premium (based on income), there is no co-payment for visits or medicines.

This tale is for people who are new to the *Caja* and the medical system here. Rule number one: Always take your *Caja* ID card and receipt showing you are paid up when you go in for attention. Whenever you find yourself standing in a line ask someone if it is the correct line for whatever it is you want to do. Even when you have an appointment with a doctor you must go through the receptionist in the area to get it confirmed (usually, too, so they can find your file). When the doctor – or anyone – gives you a piece of paper, ask what you should do with it. Any piece of paper that is for an appointment with a doctor or for a test or a prescription must have a label with your name on it. If the line is very long, make use of the phrase *"Favor de cuidar mi campo"* (please hold my place in line) and maybe you can run a few errands, or just go someplace and sit down.

On the other hand, if you are a resident, you may have a *ciudadano de oro.* This is a gold card that residents sixty-five and older can get at the Social Security office downtown. This card allows them to stand in a special line, or go to the front of lines in banks, the Public Registry, and even, I am told, at the clinics. It also is good for discounts in many stores and movie houses. I often use my *ciudadano de oro* in banks and pharmacies and the movies, but I feel guilty getting in front of people who may have more serious medical problems than I do.

Side Effects and Natural Cures

Lately it seems that I am taking more and more pills, each one for a different problem, and another one for the side effects of one of the other pills. This bothers me. When I was working, I had an assistant who was taking eight different pills, five of them to treat the side effects of the others. She became very ill and never recovered from the operation she had to have, in spite of the first pill she was taking to cure her problem. I have no doubt that her body was weakened by the interaction of all those medications.

Anyone who watches television is aware of the number of commercials for different drugs – and of all of the incredible side effects you are expected to endure in order to get relief from one ailment. The drug makers seem to think that if they list the side effects of their drugs (even if one of them is "sudden death") they are off the hook. What is also disturbing is the high cost of all of these medications. (I am beginning to wonder if the reason their drugs are so expensive is that the companies are spending so much on advertising, not research.)

Meanwhile I have been thinking of writing about the ubiquitous Ficus. This remarkable tree seems to grow in all climates, altitudes and sizes. Sandy, who grows bonsai in Tilarán, says that Ficus even make nice bonsai. I love trees. So the other day when I was downtown and walking through Parque Morazán, I stopped in front of a huge tree, first because I always notice the roots of trees, and this one had magnificent ones. Many of the roots were above ground, making wonderful spaces that reminded me of when I was little and one of my favorite pastimes was making a plan of a house at the foot of a tree, using the roots as walls. As I looked up, I saw that it also had magnificent branches. One had even grown a ridge to support another branch. I believe trees have consciousness. A little plaque stated that the tree was a *Higuerón Ficus Jimenez ll*. Really, I thought, a member of the very large Ficus family.

As I was contemplating this, a voice said something like, "Pick up a leaf." A gentleman sitting on a park bench had been watching me. I walked over to him and asked if that was indeed a Ficus. He said no, it was a *Higuerón* (fig) and the leaves gave off milk that was good for treating ulcers.

He then went on, quite passionately, to tell me that the earth grew all of the necessary cures for what ails us. That most of it was free or nearly so, but that man made drugs and charged exorbitant prices for them. In the *campo*, he said, when a dog or cat has stomach trouble, it will find a particular plant and chew the leaves, and the juice cures them. "Just watch the animals and learn," he said. (He didn't explain how to find out from the dog what was ailing him.)

And the ancients, I thought, remembering something I had read about the Indians of the Andes who chewed the coca leaf. It not only helped them survive in the rarified air; it curbed their appetite and gave them energy. Addiction was not a problem. Modern man came along, isolated the part that gave a high, and developed a drug for which we have, indeed, paid an exorbitant price. I remembered reading that the coca leaf contained Vitamin B complex, among other nutrients that seemed to prevent deleterious side effects. How many other natural medicines have we turned into drugs with harmful side effects, I wondered?

It is funny how things like that happen. I tend to believe that there are no accidents or coincidences. This chance encounter with the man on the bench was telling me something. For the moment, the mighty Ficus will have to wait for my treatise, as I am now caught up in reading about alternative treatments for ailments. It seems to me that allopathic research into the efficacy of herbal and other "natural" remedies is limited mainly to warning us about possible side effects – perhaps, as someone has said, because these treatments cannot be patented and tons of money cannot be made from them.

Costa Rica is an ideal place to do this research because the Central Market has stalls that sell medicinal herbs and there are many practitioners of naturopathic as well as homeopathic medicine here. It certainly can't hurt to check out what Mother Earth has in her medicine chest. I understand this is happening, not only here, but also in the Amazon.

Wherein Our Heroine discovers yet another Hospital

There are times when I think I'm writing a primer on the health care system in Costa Rica, or more accurately, the national medical care in San José.

A recent trip to a cardiologist at the Hospital Calderón Guardia got me a referral to a doctor in the Hospital Mexico. I had never been there before and didn't know where the bus left from San José, so last Monday I took a taxi from downtown. The Hospital Mexico is the largest hospital I have ever been in. Off long broad hallways are the various departments: Oncology, Arthritis, X-Rays, Nerve Ailments, and even one labeled "Hormones." These are large alcoves with receptions and signs so it is not difficult to find your way – and asking always helps.

At 9:00 a.m. my alcove, like all of the others, was bursting with people waiting to see one of the doctors behind the closed doors facing the rows of chairs. My doctor was Dr. Gutierrez. After promptly getting an electrocardiogram, I sat down to read the last forty or so pages of the book I had brought. I eventually wished I had brought a second book. Dr. Gutierrez had been called away on some emergency or other. By the time he showed up I was the only person in the waiting area. And then it turned out he did not have the proper machine to test my brand of pacemaker.

There was an exit closer than the one I had entered. I decided to try that one, and saw at the end of a covered walkway, a bus to San José. It took me to the south side of the *Iglesia de la Merced* – only two blocks from where my own bus stops. (I also discovered, thanks to a sign that I noticed because of the *¡Ojo!* (Look!) in large print that a bus to Immigration left from there.)

A week later I was on the crowded bus to the Hospital México, thankful to a young man who gave me his seat. This time I knew enough to take the sidewalk that led to the entrance closest to my alcove. This time it was again crowded and I learned that I should have made an appointment at the desk; that the doctor's telling me to return was not enough. But the receptionist kindly said she would tell the doctor I was here. A nice gentleman gave me his seat, telling me to "sit down" in English. It turned out that 1) he had seen my "Trader Joe's" bag and knew I was from the States and 2) he, like me, loved Trader Joe's, which began our conversation. He was there with his father-in-law, a handsome man of 84, waiting to have his pacemaker checked. The father-in-law was a Tico born in the U.S., having returned to Costa Rica and then joined the U.S. army to fight in World War II. (In fact, Costa Rica declared war on Germany even before the U.S. did.)

We compared the health services in the U.S. and Costa Rica and agreed that one reason the waiting rooms were so crowded was that no Tico comes alone. They are accompanied by at least one, and usually more, family members. And, given the sympathetic doctors and nurses here, many people take advantage of it and come in with minor ailments. "We're sissies," the older gentleman said. I pointed out that life expectancy in Costa Rica had surpassed that in the U.S. and maybe taking care of minor ailments was a form of preventive medicine.

Then the doctor came out of his office and motioned for me to enter. I was the first patient to be seen!

(That is a coup in Costa Rica, since everyone seems to have an appointment for the same time.)

Riding back to the city on the bus, we passengers got a rapid-fire lecture from a man selling little books on natural treatments and cures for all sorts of ailments. He was telling us what fruits and herbs to ingest to stay healthy. Pretty clever marketing, I thought, selling that kind of book to a captive audience leaving a hospital. I wondered. If I ever finished my book about Costa Rica, could I get on a tourist bus (for instance) and pitch it? No way, I thought, as I got off the bus holding my new purchase, a slim volume entitled *Frut Terapia* (Fruit Therapy).

Unexpected fast times at the Clínica Duran

It is said that 85 percent of medical expenses are spent during the last six months of life. That statistic used to stun me but, of course, it makes simple sense: the money is spent on some life-threatening or terminal illness (often encountered in old age) and death wins. Nobody over 70 needs statistics to tell them that they are spending more and more time seeking, waiting for, or undergoing medical attention. Some even plan their lives around their doctor appointments. You might call it an avocation of later life (although not a fun one), especially for those of us who have national health insurance.

I was scheduled to have some blood taken at the Clínica Duran and, after an experience spending ten hours in the clinic and in Hospital Calderón Guardia, I had low expectations. Armed with my book, but no breakfast, I entered the clinic a few minutes before 7 a.m. The sun was still wearing its cool color, and the air was fresh. There were few cars and fewer people on the streets. Inside the clinic I was astounded. Half of San José seemed to be here.

In the large waiting room there must have been 200 souls waiting, sitting, and standing. A cluster of people filled the hallway that led into the smaller waiting room where the lab window was. It looked chaotic. My heart sank, but soon the chaos resolved itself into different side-by-side lines.

Every time I visit the clinic I forget that no one (except myself) goes there alone. Every patient is accompanied by as many as three family members or friends. That must be why no one else brings anything to read. Once into the small waiting room, I saw that Window One had a very short line. There were only three people in front of me. After getting my paper stamped, I followed the woman in front of me to another line, one that led to the row of pews, actually, to the last row of pews. Pretty soon I was sitting down in the last pew and so I opened my book. Before I could begin to read, however, everyone in the row got up and moved along one place, the end person going to the row in front. The people in the front row moved to the front row across the aisle and then one by one into the lab.

A pleasant young man stood at the door to the lab directing the inattentive people to enter. I had to smile as I rose and shuffled along in a regular and orderly fashion. Keeping us busy kept us from getting annoyed with the wait, I figured. Once I got to the lab, the technician taking my blood was most friendly and even tried a little English on me. I, in turn, complimented her on how quickly and painlessly she did her job. Lots of experience, she explained needlessly.

I was told to return in three days to pick up the results. By 7:45 I found myself outside the clinic sipping a cup of very good café con leche that I had bought at the volunteers' table for ¢150 (about 40 cents). By now the sun was golden and it was going to be a beautiful day, all of which lay ahead of me. The only thing I had to do was remember to come back in three days' time when my test results would be ready. I stood there debating whether to take a bus downtown or a taxi home. I hadn't really made plans for the rest of the morning.

The Many Faces of Waste

Lately I have been thinking a lot about waste. I suppose it began when I heard that the U.S. government had settled upon Nevada as a dumping ground for nuclear waste and the citizens of Nevada were protesting. It does seem that with each new improvement in energy and speed there has been an increase in waste. We even have left junk in space. I wonder, does "Haste makes waste" mean that the faster we want to go the more waste products we can expect?

Did we ever worry, I wonder, about the half-life of horse manure when horses and other animals were our main sources of energy? Initially, of course, it wasn't very pleasant, but eventually it was recycled as fertilizer. Nobody wants to fertilize with nuclear waste.

Waste is an interesting word with a lot of interestingly related meanings. It can mean to destroy or devastate, it can mean to squander, it can refer to what is left over and useless, and it can even mean to kill. As I walk along (I am on my way to the Clínica Duran to keep my 7 a.m. doctor's appointment), I say, "If we continue to waste and make waste, we'll get wasted."

Once I came up with a solution to some of our waste problems. Everyone could get a compactor and turn their trash into handy little bricks, then cover the bricks with epoxy and build themselves a house with the bricks. Thus, we could live in our waste before it buries us. I have not patented this idea.

Sometimes we waste without meaning to. Some years ago I was staying with friends in Brazil and threw

159

away what I thought was an empty tube of shampoo. Their maid pulled my tube from the waste basket and showed me, by slitting it open with a razor, that I had at least three more shampoos left in that tube. To this day I wonder how much toothpaste and creams (and you name it) are left in the tubes they come in.

The route I take to the clinic begins with a shortcut down the hill on a path that is lined with garbage and tall grass, so I look out for rats and snakes. I never have seen them, but I do see again the homeless man sleeping against the last house on the hill. This route also takes me through a very poor *barrio* and, as I walk, I get annoyed with people who lament every abortion and claim that there is enough food to feed every person conceived.

Enough food is not the problem, distribution is. And even if the food were better distributed, would we be able to handle the extra waste and garbage? I think this as I see garbage bags stacked up on the street and smell the fumes from a sewer. I also wonder if there is as much lamenting over infant mortality – the babies who die from starvation, drinking polluted water, or neglect.

I arrive at the clinic, check in, open my book and settle down to wait for a while. The place is filled with people so I expect a long wait but, by 9:30, I am beginning to wonder. The doctor is seeing people who have come in after me. I go up to the desk and ask when I can expect to be seen? The woman takes some time finding my file, then tells me that my name was called but I was absent. No, my name was not called, I insist. Muttered maybe, but not called, or maybe it was pronounced so creatively I didn't understand it. The custom in the clinic is for the exiting patient to call the next person. Stuart is not easy to say for a Spanish speaker.

The clerk takes my file to a cubicle where a nurse is taking blood pressure and tells me to stand in that line, showing me by putting her thumb and index finger just a hair apart, that the wait will be short. But it isn't. The nurse takes everyone's pressure but mine. I have asked, and their appointments are for 10 a.m. I am getting annoyed.

Finally, when she takes my blood pressure, it is higher than usual. I am not surprised. I go back and sit down and the clerk again makes her finger gesture. She has put my file in the doctor's office. I expect to be called momentarily. At 10:10 I am beginning to wonder why this appointment was made in the first place. I had seen another doctor a month before and she scheduled this appointment, but she is not even here. For the life of me, I cannot think what I am going to tell this doctor. I am too angry to listen to what he might tell me, anyway, so I get up, tell the clerk, thank you, but I can't wait any longer. I march out of the clinic and stand outside wondering whether I should take a bus or a taxi home. Then I realize I am so angry that the adrenalin must be accumulating in my system. We pump adrenalin (epinephrine) when we are frightened or mad – in moments of high emotion – and it helps us in the flight or fight response. But in our modern society, it is difficult to fight or run rapidly in the other direction. I am convinced that adrenalin becomes dangerous waste in our bodies and makes us sick if we don't get rid of it. So, I decide I had better walk home – fast. As I go along, I think of the ways I can cut down on my own wasteful habits.

The Singing Patient

Having lived in several countries for varying amounts of time, I have learned to accept different realities, different ways of looking at the world that seem to work as well as my own. My way, I have found, is not always the only way – and sometimes not even the best. This makes me careful not to judge others.

After nearly five years in Costa Rica, I have learned to appreciate the fact that, although Costa Ricans look a lot like people "back home," they are indeed different, they think differently, and they have different values. So when I found myself in the Clínica Bíblica at the admissions desk registering to be admitted for a minor operation, I accepted the questions on the form as idiosyncratic, with a Costa Rican logic all their own. One was "What is your father's name?" My father died when I was five, and I am retired and living in Costa Rica. There was no way my father could be relevant to my present situation. But here family is very important, so I dutifully wrote down my father's name.

After the Admissions Officer had finished his questioning, he turned the paper around to face me and told me to sign where he had marked an X. Then he walked away. Without thinking I signed where he indicated. Under my signature was the following in English: "Should the patient fit one of these three categories": and under that in three columns were listed, "Mentally incapacitated," "Underage," "Not able to sing because of physical condition."

I smiled. The under age question explained the desire to know the father's name. As for mentally incapacitated, well, I guess the Admissions Officer had determined that when he was asking me his questions. The question about my ability to sing was another matter. But it made perfect sense to them, I am sure. Clínica Bíblica was founded as a missionary hospital. Perhaps they had choir practice for the patients. Perhaps if you were ambulatory you were expected to go from room to room caroling the less fortunate. Or maybe they used music as part of the cure. That would certainly put them ahead of my country and in the vanguard of treatment. I had read about the therapeutic benefits of music. Maybe a singing patient is a faster-recovering patient?

In the middle of my efforts to understand, I began to giggle at the thought of my singing during my operation. Had the admissions clerk left so that I could think about my capabilities? I giggled even harder. When he came back was I expected to break into song to prove my physical condition? I saw myself standing up, arms spread wide as I belted out, "The hills are alive with the sound of music!"

But the truth is, I *am* unable to sing. I can barely carry a tune. Would he accept "Row, row, row your boat"? By now I was giggling so hard I lowered my head on my arm to muffle the sound. I knew my shoulders were shaking as I tried not to laugh out loud, and I was afraid that people passing down the corridor behind me would think that some poor patient (me) was having an emotional breakdown and they would come over to comfort me. Costa Ricans might do that.

In my attempt to stop giggling, I took a deep breath, raised my eyes and started reading the paragraph above my signature. Reading always gets me out of a tough situation. This paragraph also was in English. It started out: "I sing this document with the full knowledge…"

People, Places and Ponderings

The Joys of Living Alone

Recently in Mora's Bookstore, I saw a used book by Lynn Underwood entitled, *A Woman Alone can be Contented*. I leafed through it briefly but decided not to buy it because it seemed as if it was aimed at making an unfortunate situation bearable.

I have been living alone for a long long time (by my definition, living alone means living without a family or a significant other – in short, having only yourself to consider in making decisions).

In the past decade or so, more and more people are living alone. Some by choice, others by circumstances. A good number of these people are women, and a good number of my women friends are living alone in Costa Rica. I decided to ask them how they felt about living alone here.

Many of the reasons apply in any country, like being able to eat whatever and whenever you please, getting up in the middle of the night when you can't sleep and thumping about making a cup of tea or cocoa without worrying you might wake someone – or having to say, "Can I fix you something, too?" Creating one's own routines or un-creating them at you own whim (as Sandy says). Making all kinds of noise, whether it is practicing the piano or singing off-key or having a good cry without worrying if you are driving someone crazy. All of these things are a part of the freedom one has when living alone.

As for loneliness, usually women who live alone have a variety of interests, whether it is reading, studying a language (it is a good idea for a woman alone here to become competent in Spanish), cooking, or playing at something. There are dozens of clubs here that one can join. I have found it easier to meet people here than anywhere I have lived in the States. Anyone who moves to another country has to be prepared for being lonely sometimes. I learned a long time ago that I would much rather be lonely alone than lonely with someone – I can always do something about it. And, as Margaret says, "If I'm lonely, I can always go to the phone and invite some folks to lunch."

For some of us, living alone brings a new sense of competence when you discover you can do the things that were formerly done by the man of the house, like hanging a shelf or installing a towel rack.

It is easier for a foreign woman to live alone in Costa Rica than it is for a Tica. She is not held to the customs of the country, and often she is excused as a "crazy gringa"; but, by the same token, since Costa Ricans tend to respect and be kind to older women, they look after you. That means they see you! I used to be invisible in the States. I went out today and a gentleman gave me his seat on a crowded bus and when I got off, there was another gentleman standing there with his hand out to help me. I have no problem going to a restaurant alone – I have never been seated next to the kitchen or felt ignored by the waiter or waitress.

Although break-ins and robberies are not uncommon, generally we women don't feel unsafe living alone. Some have dogs, others guards on the premises, others good neighbors.

And finally, there is the wonderful freedom to do something impulsively, suddenly decide to go out, to see a movie, or to take a nap – or even a trip.

And you have control of the TV remote. And being in control of that, the other day I tuned into an interview in progress with Barbara Feldon, formerly Agent 99 of "Get Smart." She has just written a book entitled *Living alone and Loving It.* Far more up-to-date than Lynn Underwood's book, and a title I can relate to.

New Country, New Identity

When my incoming mail indicator said I had 1,275 new messages, I began to think something was wrong. When all of the messages said, "administrator failed delivery," I knew it. I had not sent out that many messages.

I was advised the only way to get out of this predicament was to change my e-mail address. So I did. When I went back on line to my new address, I discovered no messages, everything was a blank, even, for some reason, my address book had been reduced. I was all alone. I felt that I had gone into the Witness Protection Program. A new and unknown address. No friends, no contacts. My saved messages were gone; the e-mails to answer were gone. I am, in a sense, a blank slate. And I apologize to those who were expecting an answer from me. I am hoping the Internet police get those spammers and virus spreaders in my lifetime. Meanwhile, I will have to come to grips with my new identity.

According to Ms. Streisand, people who need people are the luckiest people in the world. That is a statement that could be debated philosophically, I suppose, but right now I needed people, not to mention a bit of luck. So I decided to go to the Canada Day picnic in San Antonio de Belén. To get there I took a taxi to the Alajuela bus station and a bus to the Cariari shopping center, where I got a taxi to my final destination. A taxi from San José would have cost 4600 colones, according to my *taxista*. Instead I paid a total of 1720 colones and decided to use my savings to buy raffle tickets.

Pedregal in San Antonio de Belén is a stadium and park. A lovely site (something not unusual in Costa Rica) where a dog show was also in progress.

I paid my ¢2000 entrance fee and mingled among the crowd of friendly people (at the risk of stereotyping, Canadians seem to be a warm and friendly lot). And I met many people new to me who have been here as long as I have. Some actually recognized me, so I guess I am not entirely an unknown entity.

Inside the large building nearby were all of the raffle prizes. I was very impressed with the number of companies and groups that had given gifts to be raffled. I put my raffle tickets in the various boxes of prizes I liked but did not expect to win. I had already gained some new acquaintances, so I knew my luck would not extend that far.

Rehearsing for the Fourth of July picnic that the American Colony is sponsoring on July 3, I had a hot dog and a beer for a late breakfast. There was a program of entertainment, and Ambassador Louise Leger impressed me with her relaxed friendliness and her welcoming speech in three languages. She, like the U.S. Ambassador, will be leaving Costa Rica shortly. My sympathy to them both.

Leaving Pedregal was going to be a problem for me since there were no taxis in the parking lot. I stood near the exit and accosted people who were leaving. Eventually I found a kind soul (a friend of a friend) who could drop me off at Saretto's in Escazú, where I could catch a bus. Everyone, it seems, except me, lives on the west side of San José.

Riding home and trying to remember the names of the people I had recently met, I realized that even moving to another country is like going into the Witness Protection Program. One way or another, many ties to your old life are cut, long-standing friends are lost. And, if you want, you can even change your name and your past. But it is an opportunity to meet new people, and even become a better person, the person you always wanted to be, not just someone hiding out from the bad guys—or, in some cases, hiding out from the good guys.

Aggression and the Fragile Male

I was going to write about smiling, but the recent news of the increase in domestic violence has been on my mind. Sometimes women batter their male partners, and even kill them, but the majority of the time it is the man who uses violence or even murder to solve problems.

Esmeralda Britton, Minister of Women's Affairs, believes the increase in domestic violence in Costa Rica is due to the changes occurring in this traditionally chauvinistic society. More and more, women are working outside the home, seeking an education and becoming more independent; and men feel they are losing control. Psychologist José Ramirez says this is a simplistic conclusion; that the causes are many, including drug and alcohol abuse, or mental or emotional problems. He says it is not a gender problem.

The observation by psychologist Eric Fromm that, in some individuals, the healthy response to danger – or a situation over which one has no control – can degenerate into acts of violence, suggests that Ms. Britton's interpretation is correct. Statistics show that such individuals are more apt to be male. Not all men who abuse drugs or alcohol resort to violence. Why do some?

It is generally accepted that human males, because of hormones and upbringing, are more aggressive than human females. It is also a sad fact that violence against one's own kind, against other species and against the environment is far more prevalent among man than among

171

other primates. Women, thanks to centuries of conditioning, have learned to live their lives in circumstances over which they have no control and to live without resorting to violence. Why can't men do the same? Partly, I suppose, because during those same centuries men have been conditioned into thinking they must be in control in order to be men. Women have another trait that helps them adjust to life – the probability that they will get pregnant and discover their lives really are *not* their own; but at least this role proves them to be vital to the continuation of the species.

There are other differences between the sexes. Statistically, from conception to birth, males are more apt to suffer some form of brain damage. When this damage occurs during birth, it is my unproven theory that it is because male heads are larger and more likely to be damaged in the narrow birth canal. The neocortex seems to be the control center for our social abilities, emotions and sexual impulses. If the damage is done to this part of the brain, this control is compromised.

Male babies are more apt to be tossed in the air and involved in rough and tumble play. Both can cause damage. Males more frequently suffer from speech defects such as stuttering. Women have little problem expressing themselves, their thoughts or their feelings. I am sure many a man has thought, "If she would just shut up!" But the frustration of not being able to spar verbally with a woman or even communicate with her has probably led to many a violent act.

Without making light of this very serious problem, I keep thinking about another difference between men and women. (I am trying to counteract the depression writing about this has caused.) Women smile more often than men do. We learn to smile as babies. Smiling is a baby's secret weapon to endear himself/herself to adults. I find myself smiling a lot in Costa Rica and many strangers smile back. Friendly smiles, sympathetic or empathetic smiles, a nonverbal acknowledgement that we are all in the same human boat. Most of these smiles are from other women or girls. A smile softens the heart, but it does more than that. According to some psychologists, smiling increases the blood flow to the brain, changes the brain's temperature and even releases biochemical substances that make us feel good (are we back to phenylethylamine?). Smiling can change how you feel, as well as change how others feel towards you.

The fact is, most of us, finally, are not in control of much of anything – the incredible success of Viagra should tell us that. So we might as well just relax, smile and be happy.

(Surely I didn't say that!)

Stepping down as the Queen of Clutter is not Easy

I had started cleaning out some files and papers when I thought I was going to move. Although it felt good to get rid of some stuff, I couldn't seem to continue the campaign. I have since decided, for reasons of health, that moving right now is impossible. Then last week Mavis, dear friend that she is, again invited me to spend some days with her in the hopes that the country air of Ciudad Colon would be good for me.

Mavis has books everywhere, including on the top of the headboard of the bed I was using. Looking through the row of books, I saw one that spoke to me. (I tend to believe that things don't happen by accident.)

Eugene D'Aquili, the social scientist, wrote an interesting paper with the premise that among the imperatives that drive our lives is what he calls "the cognitive imperative," the need to create order in our world. I was thinking about this one day downtown when I stopped to look in the window of Lehmann's *Librería*. A window dresser was filling it with boxes of jigsaw puzzles. I enjoy putting them together. I like the process of creating order out of chaos – all those jumbled pieces become a picture! Then I wondered why it was that I couldn't seem to extend this pleasure to create order in my apartment. There on the shelf in the bedroom of Mavis' home was perhaps the answer: *Clear your Clutter with Feng Shui* by Karen Kingston.

We all know that clutter can make you disorganized. I have to comfort myself when I can't find something by saying to myself that I will find it when I am looking for the next thing I can't find. Kingston maintains that having clutter in the house keeps you from living life to the fullest and clearing clutter allows "fresh winds of inspiration to enter your home and your life." Who wouldn't like that? Then she tells you something that is quite helpful if you have low self-esteem about your ability to keep things neat. She says substitute the word "could" for "should" ("I *could* get rid of all of the junk in this room.") and the word "won't" for the word "can't." ("I *won't* clean the mess in this drawer right now.") These are empowering words, or at least they don't make us feel like such wimps when it comes to clutter.

Another suggestion is to make a list of all the places that are cluttered, from drawers to shelves in the kitchen to closets to whole junk rooms. Then unclutter them starting with the least (or smallest) mess to the biggest and cross off the list as you clean up. People like to cross off items on a list, she says. I like to, too, when I can find the list.

All of this fired me up so that I could hardly wait to get home to start the project. I mean, how long can you just hang out, enjoy good conversation, read, play Scrabble and have your meals served to you? It was time for action.

Sunday I returned home. First I had to get used to city noises again. No more of that Johnny two-note bird that annoyed me in the country. Instead I hear the seemingly interminable wail of the train as it proceeds through the city once again. And Monday night the roar of the crowd awakened me. I got up, wondering if they had built a stadium near me while I was gone. No, the sound was emanating from the whole city. There was a soccer game in progress and in every home and bar cheering Ticos were yelling every time Costa Rica made, or almost made, a goal. I couldn't help but smile. The accumulated sound was as if it came from a stadium.

But back to clutter: so far I have cleared out one cupboard of the jars I have been saving just in case they might come in handy. And I did throw out an old journal just to see how that felt (I rather regret that), and I have taken a couple of stacks of books to Mora's. Unfortunately, holding up my progress are all of the habits and routines I have collected that are still in my apartment. (When you go on vacation, you leave them behind.) First I am going to have to clear them out. I *could* do that tomorrow, but I probably *won't*.

Complacency is a Bad Idea

Complacency is not only a bad idea; it can be dangerous. I live in an apartment building with a daytime maintenance man and a guard at night. We have a tall fence in front with a locked gate. I have two locks on my door but seldom use both because one always seemed enough and I always had trouble coordinating them. I not only was complacent, I often was rather smug talking about how safe I was – I've even left for a month without a worry.

Yesterday I came home after lunch out – it was 3:30 in the afternoon. As I opened the door, I saw that a small part of the doorjamb was splintered. On the floor in front of me was part of the lock, some splinters of wood and lots of screws. On the dining room table were a couple of computer disks, a folder with papers and nothing else – most notably not my Toshiba laptop. It was there when I left at 10:30. I looked around. Everything else seemed normal. I walked into my bedroom. My old brown purse that I hadn't used in months was in the middle of the floor. Next to it was an old straw hat. Although my bedroom has not benefited from my clear-the-clutter mania, I knew I hadn't left either of those things in the middle of the rug.

I walked three steps to my closet. It looked like the aftermath of an earthquake. Everything that had been on the shelves was on the floor – except, as I was soon to discover, my computer carrying case and my passport.

In my still cluttered office the only things missing were the box of my back-up disks of all my columns and the book I was writing.

I have heard people whose houses have been broken into say that they feel violated. I didn't feel so much violated. I felt as if someone had taken away my life.

"Get a life," is a popular saying. Well, someone had gotten mine and now I was going to have to get another one. No passport, no computer with all my files, addresses, no back-up. I walked into the living room (by now I was feeling as empty as a person without a life could feel) and decided to watch the news to see who was worse off than I. No remote control! The cruelest cut of all.

Of course I had to report it. I can't tell others to report crimes and not do it myself. I had called in the day-superintendent, and the manager of the apartments had come, both to give me sympathy and not much more. It was 5:30. I didn't want to go anywhere, but my neighbor Ulises insisted, saying he would go with me to help with translation. Ulises Obregón is not only a neighbor and friend, he is a lawyer and I figured that couldn't hurt. The OIJ – known as "the oeejota' – is in the court building next to the new pedestrian walkway. We entered the office marked *Recepción de Denuncia*. Denouncing the thieves was the least I wanted to do to them, but it was all I could do. We took a *ficha* and sat down to wait. There were maybe a dozen people in the room before us, but I figured half were friends or family. Two people in shorts, obviously tourists, were there with two backpacks. I spoke briefly with them and learned that one of their bags had been stolen shortly after they arrived. "Welcome to Costa Rica," I thought bitterly.

After over an hour, Ulises took my *ciudadano de oro* card to the processor in the other room to see if that would speed up my complaint. It did. First a young woman took down the information, then another young woman took more particulars and told us to wait. In a few minutes she took us to another office where investigating detectives told us they would be by that evening before ten, not to touch anything.

When we got back to my apartment I insisted we have a drink (isn't that what everybody does?) and we had some snacks while we waited. A little before 10 two young detectives, one male, one female, showed up. Unfortunately, neither of the thieves had stopped to have a glass of water so they couldn't dust for fingerprints. The male detective opened a case to reveal an Olympic portable and began to type faster than I ever have. Oh, for a portable typewriter, I thought. The sum total of the evening was three pages (all with carbon copies) detailing the disappearance of my intellectual life. As I was getting ready for bed, I remembered my tape recorder, the only other thing they might have carried out unnoticed. They hadn't taken it. The reason was it was under a stack of books on my bed table. I hadn't got around to putting that in order yet.

When I first arrived here, someone (a Tico, as I remember), said that Costa Ricans are opportunists. It seems that if you don't do everything you can to keep your home safe, thieves feel almost obligated to use that opportunity to rob you.

Normal Doesn't Live Here Anymore

Friends have come to my rescue with sympathy and commiseration, and two have even offered to lend me a computer. So it is time to move on, to get on with my life and get back to normal. However, it isn't that easy. Within days of my own robbery, I was told of a friend's cousin who was shot four times when thieves stole his motor bike. He is now paralyzed.

Then my neighbor told me about his friend whose house was broken into over the weekend; the thieves poisoned the guard dog, cut the metal fence, broke into the house and emptied it of all the electrical appliances. Children are being kidnapped and killed. A retired policeman is being implicated in car theft. Enough pedestrians have been mugged on Avenida 1 to make it a dangerous place – with no police around so far to help. We keep saying, "This is not normal in Costa Rica." "Normal" doesn't exist anymore.

The sad and frightening thing I am coming to realize, is that this country, which during the 1980s was an oasis of peace in Central America, has changed. While other Central American countries were at war, this beautiful little country without an army was both safe and peaceful. It now seems as if the lawless have formed their own army. They may be unorganized, but they obviously are more than the police can handle.

Earlier today there were gunshots somewhere in the neighborhood. Once when I heard a small explosion or a loud *pop*, I knew it was just someone celebrating a holiday with firecrackers. As I listened to that *crack*, I was just as certain that it was a gunshot.

The theft of my passport, of course, required a visit to the U.S. Embassy. It is a three-bus ride for me to Pavas. Engrossed in my book, I missed the stop on the first bus and decided to walk along Calle 6 to catch another bus. After walking a block, I saw two homeless boys ahead of me; one was sitting on the sidewalk, the other, a tall skinny teenager, was standing, just looking at me. I immediately became frightened and decided to cross the street and, when a taxi came along, I hailed it. I got in, hating the idea that I had now become so fearful, even of two hungry boys.

At the Embassy in the Consular Services Section, I met others whose passports had been stolen. Some of the stories were worse than mine. One young man had come overland from the U.S. He had no trouble in Nicaragua, Guatemala or Mexico, but on his first day in Costa Rica his wallet and passport were picked out of the side pocket of his jeans, where he thought they were safe. He said, "They say that the Embassy will help you if you're in trouble or are robbed. That they will give you money. Not true. They wanted $60 before I could get a passport. When I told them all my money was stolen, they told me to contact my family."

A kindly grandmother who has been coming to Costa Rica for eight years was there with her granddaughter. When their car overheated, the nice people who offered to help stole her purse instead, then evidently followed them to the house of friends where they were staying and, when they all went to the OIJ to report the

179

theft, the thieves emptied the house of everything. When she had explained to the Embassy that she had nothing, they simply told her they needed $60 to issue her a new passport.

By now I was angry, and my anger was directed at the Embassy. My own passport, which had cost $40 to renew nearly ten years before, was now costing $60 because I had been foolish enough to get robbed. I was planning all the sarcastic and nasty things I was going to say to the Consul, if I ever got waited on. But for the moment I escaped into my book. A character in the book, a Vietnamese woman, was saying, "First you must reject hate. Hate and fear are two sides of the same coin. Hate imprisons you in time . . .   Once you let go of hate you are free of time and the past."

I read that sentence over and over. At the moment I thought I was more full of anger than hate, but obviously the two are related. I didn't want to be trapped in the past.

When I was finally in front of the Consul, I no longer was angry. I even felt a little sorry for the pretty woman on the other side of the window for all of the anger she must have to absorb.

I am just going to have to adjust to a new kind of normal.

Cowgirls Aren't the Only Ones who get the Blues

Lately I have been thinking about book titles, not the contents of the books themselves, just their titles. Such as, *Even Cowgirls Get the Blues*. That has been going through my head for a couple of days. Then I thought about *War and Peace*. Then up came the title, *The Woman Who Made Love to Men to Take the War out of Them*.

It was not until I discovered that I had assembled all of the ingredients for chocolate chip cookies on my kitchen counter that I realized that I was depressed. Even grown-up ladies get the blues. Chocolate chip cookies, as well as spaghetti with garlicky tomato sauce, are my usual defenses against the blues.

As I beat the sugar and butter together, I thought about why I was feeling so down. The irritating wind that won't quit wasn't helping. I can't hear it in most rooms of my apartment, but I can in my office. But mainly, I knew it was the news, the news from everywhere, including Costa Rica.

In the local news was the sad information that the losing presidential candidate, Rolando Araya Monge, had been beaten up by a group of celebrators – not disgruntled losers, but happy victors of the opposing party! At the same time I read that there was a drive-by shooting in Sabanilla, a suburb of San José. *Paradise Lost*, I thought. The peaceful, nonviolent beauty spot of the world that was once Costa Rica is disappearing.

The news from the U.S. is even worse. The war on terrorism looks as if it is going to expand into a world war. The powers that be know that Americans are poor readers, yet CNN now adds a moving scroll of news items different from what is being discussed and pictured. So we are expected to read one thing and absorb it as we watch and listen to something else. Enough to depress anyone, especially since the news in the crawl space is seldom mentioned above and is often more important.

Some days ago, I read in that crawl space that the testing of nuclear bombs in the 1950s has resulted in 50,000 cancers in the United States. I saw that item just once. Meanwhile, over and over I see information about all of our personal habits that can lead to cancer. More than once, moving across the bottom of the screen has been the

181

warning that women who gain more than 38 pounds during pregnancy are more prone to breast cancer. I think the government is just trying to shift the blame. One way or another, the U.S. is becoming a *Cancer Ward.*

The first batch of cookies was in the oven by now and I wondered if perhaps when I bit into one (like half the world I eat several while they are still warm), it would jog my memory of happier times, like *Madeleine* did for Marcel Proust. Hmm, that's why I was thinking of *Remembrance of Things Past.* Then immediately came to mind *Nostalgia isn't what It Used to Be*, and I realized that living in bygone days doesn't work. We have only the present — *Be Here Now*, as the title says.

I took my cookies out of the oven, and as soon as I could handle one, took it out onto my balcony and looked out over the city I love that is increasingly getting more and more polluted. Then I looked at my pitiful plants. I must do something about them, I told myself for the 50th time. I thought of *Candide* and remembered the message there. Perhaps the answer to my blues over the woes of the world about which I seem able to do so little is to cultivate my own garden.

Meanwhile I will go back into the kitchen (that is really my garden) and make a pot of beautiful red, garlicky tomato sauce. It can't hurt.

Happy Birthday, Mom

On the 14th of July, 2005, my mother was 97 years old. She was born Mickey Roda, at least I thought she was, but recently she told me her name was actually Dominica and they changed it when she went to school. Today she is known as Margaret Carlson. I think she got tired of being associated with a mouse.

Mom was the oldest of eight children of Italian immigrants. Although she was an A-student and loved school and hoped to go on to become a teacher (or – her dream future – an actress and dancer), she had to leave in the 9th grade to help care for her younger siblings. In her early teens she was married to my father, more by mutual agreement of the families than my mother's choice. Before she was 30 she was a widow facing the Depression with four children to support. She did this by opening a beauty shop in the front of our home in the village of Mayville, New York. Her shop was successful, partly because she was very good at what she did, partly because she was beautiful, charming and funny, and partly because during the Depression women continued to get their hair done – it was an inexpensive way to feel better by looking better.

I remember that, in those days, it was not unusual to see different strange, scruffy-looking men sitting on the steps of our side porch with a plate of food – a tramp or hobo, which was what we called them at that time – who had gotten off the train in Mayville. One time I recall my mother giving some of my father's clothes to a poor man. She was holding them up to see if the size would fit. They were both crying. Later one of these hopeless wanderers told me that our house was marked as a welcoming place to get a hot meal.

Mom was a strict disciplinarian, which is perhaps why I didn't appreciate how funny she was until we were both older. My sister, Annetta, who was the eldest of the three girls, got the brunt of the discipline and all of the responsibility for Donnetta and me and, as we grew older, she made sure that we did our chores. My brother Angelo was four years older and lived in another world. He kept to his attic bedroom experimenting with electricity and inventing things. For a long time, I thought he was actually a reincarnated Thomas Edison. He would fix up our radio

183

in the living room so that we could broadcast our personal talent shows from his bedroom. He also played the trombone and had a dance orchestra in high school. He was a great dancer and my dream was that one day he would ask me to dance. At seventeen he joined the Seabees and went off to the Pacific.

Movies were our favorite pastime. When Mom said no, we couldn't go to a particular movie, we three girls would tap dance into the beauty shop, do a waltz clog and belt out a song that we'd learned from Judy Garland. We ended with our pleas for movie money, also sung. If that didn't melt Mom's heart, it worked on her customers and we would happily "shuffle off to Buffalo" out of the beauty shop to the movies.

When I reached the age of 31, an age that I could remember my mother being, I forgave her every spanking, every shouted word, every mean thing. I knew I could not have done what she did. And, too, I wondered, with her beauty and her brains, what she might have been or done had her lot been different.

Since she was widowed the second time at 67, she has lived alone and kept her own house until a couple of years ago when she moved into an assisted-living residence. My sister Annetta is still taking responsibility – not only for Mom, but she also serves as the glue that keeps our family in touch.

The last time I visited Mom she was still at home, but we were beginning to worry about her forgetfulness. She knew this. I was preparing dinner for company and Mom was setting the table, complete with candles. After a bit she came into the kitchen and said, "Well, Jo, at least you don't have to worry about me setting fire to the house – I can't remember where I put the matches."

Recently Annetta told me that Mom said, "I know I am 97, but I feel 50." We both envy her. Mom is considered a member of the Great Generation. Any way you measure it, she qualifies.

Going There vs. Getting There

Sunday morning is a favorite time of mine. I watch C-Span early in the day and find out what people living in the States think. Later, there are some more interesting programs that I can watch while I do my ironing. North American writers are being featured, and this week it has been Jack Kerouac, most famous of the Beat Generation writers. People were calling in to tell of their experiences involving Kerouac or other Beat writers of the time. I was tempted to call and tell them of my own experience.

I was living in Los Angeles in a large once-elegant house with my husband and daughter. We shared the house with my brother-in-law, who owned it, and two writer friends. The three of them were publishing *Coastlines*, an avant-garde "little magazine." The house was the meeting place for poetry readings and other literary offerings.

This particular evening a group of about 25 people had gathered downstairs in the living room. They were sitting on the floor passing a jug of red wine. We were upstairs in our bedroom. A skinny young poet in blue jeans began to read his poem, and I wanted to hear it, so I went down and sat on the stairs where I couldn't see but I could hear. I was absolutely enthralled by his new poem that was entitled "Howl," and I ran upstairs to tell my husband to come listen because Allen Ginsberg had to be the Walt Whitman of our day. When he finished his reading, someone accused Ginsberg of not being sincere. He replied, "I'll show you I am sincere."

He then proceeded to take off his clothes until, I suppose, he was naked.

During this performance, most of the women ran out of the

living room and there was general bedlam. I went back upstairs wondering what the world was coming to. It was 1956.

Kerouac's *On the Road* is classified as a "road book" (no surprise there). Road books are different from travel or guide books in that they are more about the trip than they are about the destination. They include vignettes of the people one meets on the journey and observations of the customs, culture and idiosyncrasies of the people in the different stops along the way. Travelers have been writing road books since the Greek geographer Strabo. In the 14th century, Ibn Battutah wrote about his travels in Africa, Asia Minor, the Maldives and India. His observations have been an important source for historians writing about the social and cultural life of those places. Its wonderful title, *The Gift of the Beholders on the Peculiarities of the Regions and the Marvels of Journeys,* says it all.

There seem to be two kinds of people in the world. Those who enjoy the journey and those who want to get to wherever they have decided to go. (Although I fall into the first category, some of my best friends are the destination types.) With today's air travel, it is understandable that people are just anxious to get there – especially if their destination is Costa Rica.

It is really a pity that train and ship travel have become so limited. My most enjoyable trips have been via these modes of transportation. In 1990, I fulfilled part of a dream by taking a train trip from Athens, Greece to Oslo, Norway. I stopped briefly in some cities but spent most of my time on the train, talking to the people. On my trip through Germany, I talked with a gentleman who told me how he favored East Germany once again becoming part of Germany and that his son did not. He said that his generation probably felt a greater guilt about the War. In Switzerland, my seat companion explained to me why the little tool houses in gardens outside the cities were fixed up so charmingly. It seems that land is at a premium in Switzerland and many people have gardens outside the cities, but along with storing their gardening tools in these prefabricated sheds, they are using them as miniature "summer homes."

One of my favorite memories of my first visit to Costa Rica was the train trip from San José to Limón. The train took us through farmlands and mountains, over rivers and through parts of the country where there are not even back roads. We didn't go all the way to Limón. I can't even remember whether we got off in Gúapiles or went all the way to Siquirres, because we rushed to get the last bus back to San José. Whatever our destination, it was the ride that I remember. Even the ride on the packed bus back to San José was memorable for the people on it.

I am still a journey person. For me, it is the journey in life, not the destination that is important. It is the people we meet "on the road" and the experiences we have that make up the stories of our lives.

Halloween

Halloween used to be my favorite holiday. In recent years, it has given way to Thanksgiving. Here in Costa Rica Halloween was not a tradition until about forty years ago, when children started trick-or-treating and stores carried Halloween items. According to long-time resident Lillian, it was "a sweet custom" and a chance for poor children to get all the candy they wanted once. They couldn't afford masks, but they painted their faces and their parents took them around to the houses in the more affluent neighborhoods. One year the Women's Club even gave a masquerade ball as a fund raiser for charity. But eventually the *pachucos* (ruffians) got into the act of trick-or-treating and discotheques had dances that began to get pretty wild. That is when there was pressure from the Catholic Church to stop this nonsense, which it declared was a pagan celebration involving witchcraft and magic and inspired by the devil. In the Catholic religion, Halloween falls on the day before All Saints Day. I believe it is All Souls' Day. But before Christianity it was a pagan celebration.

It is interesting that when so-called witches do things that science can't explain it is called magic and evil by the church, but when a person practicing to be a saint does it, it is called a miracle and considered holy. I guess the real definition of evil doesn't have to do with the deed, but with who does it.

One of the reasons I like Halloween is the opportunity to dress up, put on a mask and be somebody else. We used to do it as kids all the time. It has been a long time since I went to a masquerade party. One of my favorites was years ago when I lived in California. The prostitutes in San Francisco held a "Hookers' Ball" on Halloween to raise money for their campaign to make prostitution legal. The year I went I made myself a toga out of curtains, wore a blond wig and a half-mask, and I carried a hand mirror. I was going as an Hetaera. Hetaerae were the courtesans of ancient Greece. The word Hetaera actually means "companion." Female prostitution was legal then, but Hetaerae and other classes of prostitutes were supposed to dye their hair blond and wear a style of clothing that distinguished them from respectable women (hmmm). In Greek art they are depicted holding hand mirrors.

Of course, not a soul knew what I was, but what was fun was my mirror. I turned it outward so people could see their faces. They were fascinated, and often startled, at what they saw. I imagined that they had donned their masks or make up, briefly looked in the mirror and then pretty much forgot that they did not look like their everyday selves.

Another masquerade party I remember was at a large, luxurious home in Sausalito. My companion at the time was a heart surgeon. We rented our costumes and I went as Catherine the Great, he went as a serf. Our host, upon greeting us, commented that inevitably, people who had money chose costumes of humble types, and people without money dressed as royalty (hmmm again).

Wearing masks of one form or another by some group or another has been a part of every culture since the beginning of time. Sometimes the mask is actual; sometimes it is a mental mask we don as we exit the door of our homes.

At any rate, walking downtown this past week I have not seen any evidence of Halloween except in the casinos. They take every opportunity to celebrate every fiesta to attract people to partake of their pagan ritual of gambling (also a universal diversion). There is, however, already plenty of evidence of Christmas in the stores and on the streets. Nobody objects to that, although Christmas is another Christian holiday that was superimposed on a pagan celebration.

A Semana Santa Visit with Mavis

As beautiful as this country is, living in Costa Rica for me is more about friends than it is about places. I no longer have a need to visit the beaches and rain forests, but when it comes to friends, well, I can see them over and over again.

I knew who Mavis Biesanz was long before we met. Her first book on Costa Rica, *The Costa Ricans,* was my reference for learning about the culture and people. When we finally met, I felt a bit intimidated, but we seemed to have a lot of things in common. To begin with, we both grew up in the snow belt of the United States (and I loved her book, *Helmi Mavis: A Finnish-American Girlhood,* which is about growing up in Minnesota).

We both had more than a passing interest in anthropology. It was my major in college, and much of *The Costa Ricans,* the latest edition of which is called *The Ticos,* written with her son and daughter-in-law, Richard and Karen Biesanz, is cultural anthropology.

We both were sort of goody-two-shoes academic achievers. Mavis outdid me here. She graduated from college *summa cum laude* while working at four jobs. I managed a "With Distinction" and only one job. And finally, we both love to play Scrabble.

So when she invited me to spend the week before Easter at her home in Ciudad Colon, I said yes. Normally, Easter Week is a very quiet, solitary time for me. The world seems to have gone to the beaches, and I am left with a peaceful San José, but little else. This would be different.

It *was* different. Peaceful, totally relaxing, with little to do but enjoy ourselves (which meant we read, talked a lot and played a lot of Scrabble). I didn't even have to cook. Mavis' son's Thai cook Som Kid sent us meals for the week. (You can imagine my confusion and thoughts when first she said, "Som Kid will be bringing our meals." "Any idea which kid?" was nearly my response.)

One day Bill White, our special and mutual friend, who founded the Julia and David White Artists' Colony in Ciudad Colon, invited us to lunch at his new house. He built it above the tennis court, and it is a joy of country living. His assistant Ron and I are trying to convince him to replace the virtually unused tennis court with a bocce ball lane and perhaps a racquet ball court.

On another day, after a short walk, as we were about to enter Mavis' house, a tall pretty woman with auburn hair suddenly appeared and began speaking to us in Spanish. She explained that she had been watching a family of iguanas and felt as if she were living in a prehistoric park.

Christina turned out to be German (we soon switched to English) and Mavis' new neighbor. In the middle of their moving in she invited us for a visit (I could never have done that), and we had a glass of wine with her, her husband Martin and their son, Douglas.

Martin is the new rector of the University for Peace. I am thrilled that finally the University for Peace is actually functioning as a university and is in the hands of someone who is both a visionary and pragmatic. (I know that sounds like an oxymoron.)

On my last day, Mavis and I went out to Grecia, where many more friends had gathered at Ruth's to say farewell to Bonnie and Arnold. Ruth no longer is in the organic pineapple business, but when she was, she and Norma produced the sweetest, most delicious pineapples I have ever tasted.

Bonnie and Arnold came to Costa Rica as Peace Corps workers and stayed on for the next 10 years to spend part of the year in the village where they had volunteered. They are going back to California more or less permanently and I am going to miss them. However, it was one good farewell party.

So that was my *Semana Santa*. I discovered something that doesn't take a philosopher to learn: spending time with friends really beats spending a week alone, no matter how quiet and tranquil the latter may be.

Wedding Bells for the Two Sandys

Two of my dearest friends in Costa Rica are getting married. Sandy S. is marrying in January and Sandy C. in February. Both women have been members of my writing group over the years, and I admire them beyond expression.

Sandy S. came to Costa Rica in 1990 with her then-husband. They bought some property near Grecia with the hopes of starting a bed and breakfast. Being in the country, the property had plenty of banana trees. Sandy learned to make dozens of recipes calling for bananas, which were always threatening to over-ripen and overwhelm. Other than producing a charming manuscript of her experiences, the bed and breakfast venture was not a success, so the property was sold and Sandy moved to northern Costa Rica with an abiding aversion to bananas.

When her marriage broke up, Sandy went through a number of years establishing herself as a person in her own right (coming into a *machista* culture with a husband, a woman becomes an official appendage, with everything in her husband's name). While doing this, she studied Spanish, *really* studied Spanish. While I am still speaking kitchen Spanish, Sandy speaks it well enough to teach it (which she does) and to do translations—including a book of poetry.

Then she decided to become a citizen of Costa Rica, a country she has grown to love. Becoming a citizen is not easy; it requires in-depth information about the country's history, government, topography, as well as knowledge of arcane Spanish grammar, not to mention written and oral fluency in the language. Sandy passed on the first try.

For relaxation, since she loves to ride, Sandy raised a couple of horses and has ridden in some local *topes*. As a citizen, she has become involved in local environmental issues. In the course of all of this, she met Roger, another expat, and a talented and versatile craftsman. After some years of a growing friendship, and supporting each other through tough times and celebrating the good times, the two are getting married.

Sandy C. has probably visited and lived in more countries than any secretary of state. The difference is in the way she traveled and how she lived. I don't understand how she is not constantly jet-lagged. She lived in a Chicago ghetto in fear of her life during the uprising in 1968. She and her husband and daughter were the only white family in a black neighborhood in the American South. She lived for years in Africa, keeping house in conditions that even Peace Corps volunteers wouldn't envy – like the primitive apartment over a noisy bar in an African village. She has shivered in a cold-water flat in Belgium, and enjoyed only slightly more comfort in Australia. Sandy lived in these places because she worked for NGOs (non-government organizations), often trying to repair the damage that industrial countries thoughtlessly wreak in the Third World. Or she was just trying to help with problems overlooked by local governments.

After her marriage broke up, Sandy moved to Costa Rica and became a consultant to NGOs as well as other organizations that seem to have lost their vision. The lessons Sandy has taken during her life's work have made her one of the wisest women I know. She is one of the few people who could honestly say, "Do as I do," and not just "as I say." Her wisdom, like all good wisdom, is laced with love. She knows how to nurture friendships, and takes the trouble to do it. She has single-handedly established "traditions" here in Costa Rica with some of these friends: a Christmas luncheon every year for our writing group, and a regular "Gourmet Hot Dog Dinner" with those of us who love hotdogs, are just two that I know of. Sandy's writing tends to essays about her experiences, especially with people she has met in villages in Africa. There is a spiritual dimension to all she writes.

After living for years in a difficult marriage in impoverished conditions (partly as a result of her choice of work), Sandy now lives very comfortably in Costa Rica and, not to sound corny, has found romance with Harry (they met at a dance, which I think is very romantic). Although coming to it from a different route, Harry shares her desire to help others help themselves, and they do this together through a foundation Harry has established. They are getting married on Valentine's Day.

As much as I have always loved other people's weddings, I can't attend either, but I will be thinking of them both with a lot of love on their special days.

Those Tiny Things that go ZZZZ in the Night

It is not just the *escarabajos de mayo* that introduce the rainy season. One of the nice aspects of living where I do (in a third floor apartment in the city) is that I seldom see the various flying insects my friends in outlying areas do. It is rare that a fly will find its way into my apartment, moths only occasionally, and mosquitoes almost never.

But at the beginning of the rainy season I, too, am visited by those *escarabajos,* which I call dumb bugs because they bump into things and, if they land on their backs on the floor, that's it for them unless a kind human comes along and rights them or throws them out into the night. (Time out while I take the dumb one clinging to the cushion on my couch out to the balcony.) They are not dangerous, just a nuisance.

It is the *zancudos* that make me crazy. *Zancudo* is the Latin American word for mosquito but, according to my friend Anabel, the *zancudo* is a special mosquito that comes about this time of the year to let you know that the rains are on their way. The problem is, they wait until the middle of the night to do this and want to whisper (or zzzzz) their announcement in your ear on their way to biting you.

Lately I have been waking up boxing my own ears. Then I got a citronella candle and for two nights that worked, although burning a candle while I slept seemed a bit dangerous. On the third night, when the candle was low, the current *zancudo* was undeterred and I was back to boxing my ears and then sleeping with the sheet over my head.

I have learned that "walking a mile in someone else's shoes" is really hard unless "the shoe fits" (to combine a couple of old metaphors). My husband was allergic to mosquito bites. I was not. He would wake me in the middle of the night, all lights blazing, as he searched the room for that elusive mosquito that had been biting and pestering him. Maybe they only go after those who are allergic to them, because they didn't bother me at the time. With ill grace, not at all understanding his obsession, I would get up and help him look. The elusive mosquito was usually in the fold of a curtain. Now I understand his obsession.

Recently I read that researchers are discovering that birds are really smart. Some birds have even taught themselves how to use tools. Just watching my little sparrows getting me to feed them, I discovered birds were smarter than we give them credit for. They cinched my conviction when one day they dragged the empty seed bag into the living room from behind the door on the balcony.

When I was studying anthropology, humans were so smug about our superiority and the gap between us and other animals, that any research that was done was flawed by this assumption. Just about everything that animals did was attributed to instinct, in spite of those animals, isolated in cages, who behaved so differently from animals in their natural habitat.

Now I really doubt that humans are the best that evolution (or God, if that is your belief) can do. There is not such a great gap between us and other animals. I am waiting for studies to extend the intelligence they have found in birds and in other animals to mosquitoes. I am also waiting for the discovery that other animals – including mosquitoes – do laugh. Scientists will probably stop there, not eager to learn what it is they are laughing about – or at.

A Few Cures for Rainy-Day Blues

When I compare our weather to the rest of the world, I really can't complain, but I'm getting rather tired of this unseasonably cold weather. I want my sunny mild-to-warm days back. Instead I get clouds full of rain. Many years ago when I was living in Cambridge, Massachusetts, it rained for something like seventeen days in a row, and to keep my sanity I made a little booklet of seven ways to kill yourself in the rain. Instead of that, over the past weeks I have been coming up with ideas of what to do in San José (short of killing yourself) when it is cold and/or rainy.

One choice, of course, is to stay home and clean out the refrigerator. Once you close the refrigerator door, the rest of the room feels warm. Another (the one I prefer) is to stay home in bed under the covers and read a good book. What a luxury. One especially good book to read is *Helmi Mavis: A Finnish American Girlhood* by Mavis Biesanz. San José will seem downright toasty after a winter of blizzards and snowdrifts in Tower, Minnesota. For those of us over sixty-five, it will bring back many memories.

Another pastime is cooking. If you love to cook as I do, trying out a new recipe is a great idea on cold and rainy days. I suggest something that requires baking. That way the kitchen warms up a bit – or, in the case of my stove, a lot. After you have finished, find a reason to sit in front of the open oven. Here is a great recipe for a rainy day:

Real Gingerbread

½ cup butter
½ cup water
1 ½ cups flour
½ cup *tapa dulce en polvo* (or light brown sugar)
½ tsp salt
3 TB ginger, minced
1 tsp. baking soda
1 egg
¼ cup corn syrup
1 cup raisins (optional)

In a large saucepan, heat water and butter enough to melt butter without letting the water boil. Remove from the heat, stir in *tapa dulce*, corn syrup, then egg and ginger. Combine baking soda, flour, salt and raisins and beat into liquid mixture.

Bake in well greased 8-inch baking pan at 350 degrees (180C) for about 35 minutes, or until the gingerbread has shrunk a little from the sides. Frost with cream cheese frosting or serve as is.

If you still have a lot of ginger left over, peel it, chop it and store it in a jar filled with enough sherry or vermouth to cover. It will last for months in the fridge.

And there's always a movie – if you can stand the air-conditioning. Assuming you can't persuade theater managers to turn it off, even though it is even chillier outdoors, make sure you wear a warm sweater and shoes with socks. Or better still, rent *Towering Inferno* and watch it at home.

You can always watch television, but not just the regular fare you usually watch. Surf the channels a bit; expose yourself to different languages. Brush up on your Spanish with one of the local channels (with dictionary in hand) or watch the Italian station, which has a way of warming the heart, if not the feet.

Keep in mind, I am talking about an apartment that has no heating facilities, something I used to brag about to my U.S. friends and family. I have neither air conditioning nor heating, both of which I dislike, and neither of which I need. That's what I used to declare. I am not exactly eating my words right now, but I am warming them up. Friends who live outside the city have suggested that all I have to do is hop a bus and go downhill several hundred meters to a place like Ciudad Colon, or even to the beach, and experience a tropical climate. But that would be giving up.

Finally, I suggest that you take some of what you baked to your nearest friend who has a fireplace. I can't imagine anything nicer on one of these coolish, rainy days than sitting in front of a fireplace with a hot cup of tea or coffee, chatting with a good friend and munching gingerbread.

More Rainy Day Blues

About three years ago we went through an early rainy season that was both cold and wet, and I wrote about things to do to fight the blues. We are again experiencing seasonal rainy days. We have been having some real *aguaceros* (downpours) this past week and I have been getting a real case of the blues. Mainly because after each rainfall I discover my bedroom flooded, the water accumulating under the bed and near the door. Mopping up an inch of water is not one of the cures for the blues I had in mind.

The last time I had a flood was when I was living in a three-bedroom, wall-to-wall carpeted apartment. It was after an earthquake that didn't do much damage, except for a broken pipe, which left the entire apartment under an inch of water that I spent two days sweeping into the one drain in the kitchen. It left me with a terrible backache and, mopping up my bedroom now, I am haunted by this memory.

The first time I came home to discover the water, Dannys, our maintenance man, told me the rain had come in through the open window. So the next day I closed my windows before leaving. I came home to a flooded bedroom. (How thankful I am that I no longer have a carpet!) The next day I stuffed towels on the windowsills. I came home to more water, still under the bed and far from the windows. On the fourth day I lined the baseboards with towels, thinking it was coming in through some crack the tilers had left, because the only change in here since the last rainy season has been the new floor tiles.

That day I came home during what I thought was a light rain and discovered my bedroom flooded again. I called Dannys. He told me there had been a strong rain around the apartment. In Costa Rica I have watched it rain across the street while I was standing dry. Once again, the only water on the windowsills was a bit on the small louver window, but no water on the floor beneath it – only in front of the inside wall and under the bed. This time Dannys did the mopping, both of us baffled by the location of the water. I felt like I was in a Sherlock Holmes mystery

Then, before he had finished, the rains came again – another *aguacero* – and the two of us watched as the large outside drain pipe visible from my bedroom began to shoot water into the room with the force of a fire hydrant. The water came in through a small hole in the corner of one of the louvers, overshooting the sill and landing on the floor near the far wall and accumulating under my bed.

It turns out that when some workmen were doing something on the apartment above they somehow separated the drainpipe at the joint. The water gathered, then, with the help of the wind and the direction of the drainpipe, it came pouring into my apartment. Mystery solved. I just hope all of this rain helps to fill our cisterns so that the water shortage is alleviated. Storing it in my bedroom doesn't cut it.

When it's Time to Move On

One of my favorite books, *The Once and Future King,* has some advice I often think of. Merlin tells the young Arthur, "When you feel sad, learn something new."

My daughter Lesley and I went to see the movie, *The Italian Job.* Someone (probably the hero) tells the heroine, who is still grieving for her dead father, "It's time to move on." Moving on is like learning something new. It has become a popular phrase and will no doubt get over-used pretty soon. Perhaps it started with the web site, moveon.com, which was created during the relentless and seemingly endless investigation of President Clinton. It meant, "Enough already, let's get on with life, let's talk about (and learn) something new."

Lesley and I were discussing this idea of moving on after the movie. She remembered the time when I was still living in San Jose, California, and told her about seeing this incredible dining and living room suite in a second-hand furniture store. It was all glass and chrome, which I normally don't care for, but the padded dining chairs not only swiveled but were on wheels. I could describe the rest of the furniture in great detail but will spare you and Lesley. It was marked at $1000 for the whole thing. I wanted it badly and passed the store almost daily to gaze in the window to see if it had been sold yet. I dreamt of where I could possibly put it because my job was a live-in situation and there was no room for it in the International House. According to Lesley, I carried on about that furniture for years and, in retrospect, she wished she had had the phrase, "It's time to move on, Jo." A polite way of saying, "I'm sick of hearing about that damn furniture."

Of course, that is not the only occasion I have been stuck in time by something I have done or something that has happened to me that I couldn't get over. Years ago at a New Age Fair I picked up a book by an Israeli guru. I can't remember the title or author, but I do remember one bit of advice on how to get beyond hurts – the slings and arrows often wielded by others – that obsess us. In my case, it was an old love affair, which was always interfering with my thoughts and energy. What the author said to do was get in the shower, turn it from hot to full-blast cold and, while standing under it, yell, "I forgive you, _____!" and name whoever or whatever has wronged you. Stand there and say it as long as you can. I tried that. It took three different showers but, after that, I was able to move on with my life without thinking of Jack. It was a great relief and I have since given this advice to my friends, none of whom has wished to follow it.

One thing is sure, the world continues to turn and the days continue to pass even if you are stuck in a yesterday. Recently, Lesley told me a story she heard from a Weight Watchers member. At a Monday morning meeting, an extremely distraught woman confessed to the group that she had eaten an entire Sara Lee cheesecake the night before. Everyone groaned in empathy. "I need to know," the cheesecake eater said, "how many points I have to cut out this week to make up for that cheesecake." (In Weight Watchers, foods are given different points and you are allowed a certain number of points a day, usually somewhere in the twenties. A cube of cheese might be 4 points, but the good news is any amount of green vegetables counts as zero.)

"Oh, you really can't make up for it," the leader said. "There is more than a week's worth of points in an entire cheesecake. Just get back on track and stay within your point range for the rest of the week."

"No," the woman said, "I need to offset the points."

"You can't possibly reduce your daily points enough to make up for the cheesecake." The leader repeated.

"There must be something I can do about that cheesecake," the woman wailed. The two of them went on like this for some time. It was clear that nothing short of complete absolution was going to satisfy her. Finally, out of sheer frustration, the leader threw up her hands and said, "Look, just count it as a vegetable and move on!"

That, I have decided, will become my mantra when I find my mind stuck on something I regret but cannot change. I will just count it as a vegetable and move on.

The Bottoms of my Socks

My friend Lillian suggested that I write about the bottoms of my socks. It all began during a telephone conversation when she asked me how I liked my new tile floor (everybody is asking me). I told her that I loved it. At first, I wasn't sure that I would because instead of the typical foot-square tiles, they had installed tiles that measured eighteen inches on each side. I'd never seen those in a house; in a supermarket, maybe, or a hotel, but not a medium sized apartment. The tiles are light beige marbled with darker shades of rosy brown. I had a friend who was an interior designer and thus knew the names of many colors, hues and tones, and she could describe things so vividly. I am sure she saw things differently than I did. Anyway, I love getting out of bed and walking barefoot on the cool clean rosy tiles.

Usually at home I wear white socks. I started doing that when I realized that wearing shoes made my floor dirtier. If I spilled some water on the floor in the kitchen, my shoes turned it into a spot of dirt. My white socks just dry it up. My old tile always seemed to be dirty, and no matter how often I mopped it (mainly just where I walked), the bottoms of my socks were black by the end of the day. I knew this was not inevitable because when I visit my sister in Florida or my daughter in California, my white socks are still clean at the end of the day. It was getting to be a chore trying to keep my floors clean. Not to mention that each week I had at least one load of laundry of nothing but white socks with black bottoms.

Then, thanks to my neighbor Hilda, I found a maid. Actually, in Costa Rica, where the concept of equality is very important, household helpers are not called *criadas,* which is the word for maid in Spain, they are called simply *empleadas,* or employees. So now I have an employee to help me keep my new tiles clean.

Roxanna is good-natured and hard working. She mops the whole apartment, polishes my furniture, cleans out my cupboards and, in the fashion of all *empleadas,* never puts anything back where it was.

Some advice I have gotten regarding household help here is "never fix their lunch." Lillian could never go to lunch on Mondays because she had to fix lunch for her maid. So when Hilda told me that part of the deal was to fix Roxanna's lunch, I feared the worst. Roxanna started working four hours on Thursday mornings, but soon asked if she could come two days a week, so now she works three hours each on two days.

She can't eat what I often do (whatever I have in the fridge); I have to make sure she gets some protein, a starch and a vegetable. And she can't eat the same thing over and over, as I sometimes do. On days Roxanna doesn't come, I plan her menu and do the shopping. Then Hilda had to go and tell me that Roxanna was raving about the lunches I prepared for her. I wish she hadn't told me that. Now I find myself trying to outdo the last lunch.

So there I am, hard at work in the kitchen fixing lunch while Roxanna is hard at work in the rest of the apartment, mopping and polishing. After she has left I pad around my clean apartment, loving my new tile floor even more. I just can't understand why, at the end of the day, the bottoms of my white socks are still dirty.

Reading *The Kitchen Boy* in Escazú

Mavis invited me to a meeting of her Book Club. I call it "her" Book Club because she has been the chair of it for so many years. Actually, the Book Club is an interest group of the Women's Club and was active in 1971 when Mavis settled in Costa Rica and joined.

Book clubs are one of my favorite things. I first was introduced to them when I was a very young faculty wife at Gettysburg College. A Book Club existed there but it was only for full Professors and their wives, so my instructor husband and I were not eligible. They met on Saturday nights (so you can imagine what college professors did back then). My husband and I, along with other younger and less titled faculty, formed our own Book Club and we met on Friday nights. Our books were a little jazzier than the ones the full professors read. Like the other Club, we had one person who would give a book review. Sometimes the rest of us would have read it. The only book I remember from then is *Comes the Comrade*, the story of a woman in, I think, Czechoslovakia, whose estate was taken over by the Russians. The reason I remember it is that she would get up early in the morning and walk around her estate smoking her morning cigarette. That was the only time she felt free. So I began getting up at 6:00 a.m. and walking around the block where we lived, smoking a cigarette, feeling free. Faculty wives were under close observation in those days, but not many observers got up that early.

It was many years before I joined another book club. I was living in San Jose, California. This was co-ed, too, and we met once a month. In this case, we all read the same book and discussed it. As in the first club, the hosts served a late supper. I never missed a meeting except for something dire. I told my daughter about my book club (it was called Ex Libris) and she immediately organized one in Pasadena, California. Hers has been going for over ten years. The hostess (it is all women) makes dinner. Over the years the dinners have become more and more elaborate. One time when I was visiting and Lesley was the hostess, the book was *Chocolat,* so we prepared a French dinner. Once a year they spend a weekend at the beach eating and talking books (I *think* they talk about books).

Most of the book clubs I know about have had fewer than ten members; not so with the Women's Club. Although it started small, it has grown to some twenty-three members. The first book that Mavis was asked to review was her own, *The Costa Ricans.* (The precursor of the latest Biesanz book, *The* Ticos.) Because nobody wants to quit this group, natural attrition seems to be the only way members leave. The Book Club meets once a month at a member's house. They meet in the late morning and stay for lunch. One person reviews a book that others may or may not have read. The hostess prepares the main dish and others bring the rest. Usually at least 18 people show up.

The oldest member, Norma, has just celebrated her 90th birthday. Norma has become a model for all of us women who hope to achieve her age: she is pretty, vital, vivacious, immaculately turned out and more active than most of us.

This week the meeting was held at Mavis' new home high in the hills above Escazú. Rhoda Oblensky reviewed *The Kitchen Boy*, a fictional tale of the exile and imprisonment of the royal family of Russia. During the discussion Mavis mentioned a book she is reading titled *Reading Lolita in Teheran*. This book is about a group of women in Iran who meet at their professor's home (creeping there in their burkas, and risking arrest). Once there, they throw off their burkas and read and discuss great books of the West. She (the professor) lost her job when the universities were closed in Iran but wanted her female students to continue to read and learn.

It sounds like a fascinating book and just goes to show to what lengths people will go to belong to book clubs.

Science Catches up with the Past

When I went back to college in the 70s, one of my classmates in anthropology kept going on about a new concept in the social sciences called "systems theory." I had no idea what he was talking about. It seemed to have something to do with computers and networking.

I listened enrapt, but I have a totally unscientific mind, and the closest I could get was Einstein's Theory of Relativity, thinking he was talking about how everything was related. Later, when there was much talk about new paradigms, I remembered my friend and what he claimed was a new way of looking at the world via systems.

Some time later I went to a lecture by the author of the *Tao of Physics* and listened to Fritjof Capra talk about a new way of viewing things scientifically. Instead of looking at a unit such as an atom and trying to analyze it and figure out its function, physics was beginning to look at that unit in relation to other units and its surroundings. You could only get information about something by its interaction with other somethings. Everything was part of a system. This was the new concept. No more looking at isolated atoms.

More of this came home to me when I was helping Chinese students practice their English. One of them, a doctor, told me how Chinese medicine was different from Western medicine. One of the differences was they did not look at the various organs of the body as separate entities that they were going to treat; rather they saw and treated organs as parts of a system. Thus they consider the kidneys, lungs and heart all as part of one system and treat them as such. Chinese medicine, as a result, is more apt to look at the entire unwell person, not just a diseased liver.

And then last Sunday I was listening to Jan Hoffman of *The New York Times* on C-Span talk about the *Times'* printing obituaries of all of the people who were killed in the Twin Towers disaster. She said that when she called family members to ask about the life of the person who had been killed, they never talked about the job he or she did, they talked only about that person's relationship to others, their role as father, mother, friend, child or loved one. They never mentioned the victim's work, only what he/she had meant to others.

In a way, I thought, scientific societies have come full circle. Most traditional societies, and certainly Costa Rican society, have always known (and never forgotten) how important systems are, systems such as family or a group of friends, a neighborhood, a community. The poets also have long known this and John Donne said it very simply: "No man is an island."

Sometimes I Think in Quotes

Someone once said that every movie, even a bad one, had one good quote. There are some lines that come to mind such as, "Make my day," or "*Hasta la vista*, baby." But I was thinking more along the lines of "Fasten your seat belts, it's going to be a bumpy ride." Or, "Frankly, my dear, I don't give a damn." Or Robert Mitchum's comment in a war movie, "Only the uniforms and the transportation change." Of late I tend to be reading more books than seeing movies and I have found myself thinking about certain lines I have read in the past weeks. I haven't been able to figure out why some ideas stay with me at any particular time. Of course, one person's quote is another person's throwaway line.

One that struck a chord with me was E.M. Forster's comment in *Howard's End*: "It is the vice of a vulgar mind to be thrilled by bigness." That made me think of Costa Rica where almost everything, beginning with the size of the country, is small. When I moved here, there were few really big department stores, but plenty of little boutiques, no large drug stores, but plenty of small *farmacias*. One or two really large restaurants and dozens of small *sodas* (mom and pop restaurants), some of them with only two or three tables. One or two big supermarkets but plenty of *pulperías,* crowded little grocery stores that remind me of the corner store of my youth (why are they so often on corners?). Indeed, in Costa Rica, "small is beautiful" fits a description of the country.

But things are changing and soon "bigness" will be as much a part of Costa Rica as it is of other countries. We now have PriceSmart and Office Depot. Even Mora's Bookstore, which used to have books crowded to the rafters in a fourteen-foot storefront, has doubled in size (and the books still go up to the rafters).

In her mystery novel, *Death in Holy Orders*, P.D. James has a character say, "We all have our own resources for staving off those two horrors of human life, boredom and the knowledge that we die." The resources he mentions are football, shopping, art, music, travel, alcohol and drugs and even the Internet. And one could add sex and gambling. This little country is filled with "resources" to stave off those two horrors, which loom ever closer to those of us who are retired and must restructure our lives.

And finally, good old Marcel Proust, a writer whose books I have been trying to read for years. Actually it is Diane Ackerman, in her book, *The Natural History of Love,* who quotes Proust: "We do not love people for themselves . . . we alter them incessantly to suit our desires and fears." Then either Ms. Ackerman or Proust adds, "It is only because we need people in order to feel love that we fall in love with people." I might quibble with that statement. Not with the idea that we need people; I believe we do (although, to quote Jean Paul Sartre, "Hell is other people."). It is just that I think people with pets would argue that they don't need other people in order to love; they only need another breathing living organism that can love them back. I could argue that we don't need either. We could become passionately in love with a place, with an idea, with a chosen course of work. And the passion we feel for these things can spread to others. However, it is the first part of the quote that caught my eye and thoughts. We do tend to attribute to the ones we fall in love with all sorts of virtues they really don't possess. Usually we don't realize that the one we loved does not have the qualities we attributed to him until we fall out of love and we wonder what we ever saw in him to begin with. (Meanwhile, our friends never could see the attraction in the first place.)

I know it is possible to see in a place (a city, for example) what we wish to see, and to obliterate what we don't want to see. I read the article in the *New York Times* about gambling in Costa Rica. The San José the author described in most unflattering terms is not the San José I know. But then, in his short visit, Mr. Berlind didn't fall in love with the city. Which reminds me of another quote, the origin of which I have completely forgotten. It seems silly, but I think it is really profound: "We love what we love."

The More Things Change, the More I Object

Legend (or perhaps history) has it that President Lincoln asked his speechwriters to come up with a phrase that would suit all occasions. I can't tell you how far and wide they searched – this, after all, is not a fairy tale – but sooner or later they came to him with the phrase he could use as a universal response: it was "And this too shall pass."

What this phrase also says is that change is inevitable. When you're a kid that thought may be a comfort, if you think about it at all, but you are so preoccupied with the changes you yourself are going through you don't notice outside changes. But as an adult whose ways and life are pretty much established, outside changes are not always welcome. (I am not even going to deal with the changes we notice in ourselves – also unwelcome.) Sometimes it is not true that "The more things change the more they stay the same."

I was thinking about this the other day while walking downtown. The biggest change I have noticed in San José is the number of cars – on the streets, in the parking lots, in showrooms, blocking sidewalks. Getting downtown by taxi is to be stuck in gridlock. Walking is worth your life crossing the street since cars, by dint of their sheer weight, and the lack of experience on the part of many drivers, claim the right of way. I've also noticed that there are a lot of new very large buses on the streets. Many of these buses seem to exude fewer black emissions. That is good. Even with the greater number of cars, the buses seem to be pretty full. So the streets are filled with loaded buses and cars with one person in them – most of them standing still. The advantage of having the freedom of movement as the result of having your own car has reached a point of diminishing returns in this city whose streets are not equal to the challenge.

I have also noticed the increase in the number of fat people. When I first came here, I didn't see one obese person on the streets. I was particularly struck by this, because every time I returned to the States from another country the first thing I noticed was that Americans were fatter than most other people of the world. Now there are a lot more fat people on the streets in San José. There are many reasons for this, I am sure, including the influx of people from other countries. But I am also sure the advent of so many cars and more TVs, in addition to more and more fast food restaurants, have contributed to the extra weight pounding the streets. In a column on this subject, fellow columnist Laureen Diephof says that research done by the United States Department of Agriculture shows the size of food portions in fast food restaurants has doubled in the past 25 years. A small order of French fries is bigger than the large size of the past. I've noticed that in many restaurants here, the portions are larger than they used to be.

My e-mail friend Enrique caught me up to date on the changes in Mallorca and Spain. Other than the cost of living that has gone up, he tells me that there are huge bulldozers in Alicante and other places digging up the land bordering the sea to put up skyscraping condominiums which, of course, block the view of the sea for others. For many of us, change seems to result in a loss in the quality of life.

And finally we come to what really prompted these musings. My favorite chocolate candy, Gallito's *Milan Relleno*, used to be a delicious little dark chocolate log filled with chocolate mint. I used to take them back to the States as presents and eat at least one a day. Recently they changed the packaging to a lighter green and silver for no reason that I could figure, except that with the change came a difference in the quality of the chocolate. It simply is not as good. That's the bad news. The good news is I am no longer addicted to this candy. I can take it or leave it.

If all of these changes too, shall pass, I wonder what I am going to object to next.

If the World were according to Stuart

Humans are definitely not the end of the evolutionary line. If we were, we would have four arms, not just two. I think about this every time I have to put down my two bags of groceries in order to turn the key and the knob of my front door simultaneously.

Even before we came down from the trees (assuming early humans were once arboreal), life would have been easier with four arms. I thought about this again the other day when I was downtown and saw a man carrying a brief case, trying to talk on a cell phone and open an umbrella all at the same time.

Speaking of cell phones, drivers on cell phones would not be such a hazard to others if they had four arms. Come to think of it, a Lamarckian could argue that the ubiquitous use of cell phones will eventually promote the evolution of a human species with four arms.

Joy would be added to life. Just think of the din of appreciation that would follow a performance of our wonderful National Orchestra if we had four hands to clap with. (And imagine a piano concerto!) If she had had four arms, the Smothers Brothers' mother could have hugged both of them at the same time, and avoided all that sibling rivalry. As a matter of fact, all mothers could use four arms. How often has a mother said, "You'll have to wait, I only have two hands, you know." Hugging might become an art form.

If we had four arms, we could be a lot more efficient. Ticos could wash their hands and brush their teeth at the same time during lunch hour (and maybe the rest of us would pick up the habit). Politicians would be able to shake twice as many hands during their campaigns — or would they be shaking hands and reaching into our pockets at the same time? A traffic policeman could direct all four corners at once. A surgeon would not have to say, "Scalpel, please." He/she could get it him/herself. (The English language isn't perfect, either). Roulette players could place twice as many bets before the croupier calls, "*No más apuestos. Manos afuera!*" Croupiers could gather the chips faster (we could all lose money faster). Bridge players could sort their cards much faster and thus get more games in on a rainy afternoon.

I could be typing this and eating my lunch at the same time.

Of course, there is always a downside to great ideas. Having four arms would be of absolutely no use to soccer players (who might even argue that four legs would be more desirable), but think of all the other sports having four arms would benefit. Learning which arm to put in a sweater first would take twice as long. President Bush would have even more problems with pledging allegiance to his flag, and pickpockets would probably flourish even more than they do today.

Like all great ideas, this one is not entirely new. Perhaps having seen into the future, the Hindu god Shiva has multiple arms. Of course, Shiva also has a third eye. I will think about the advantages of that and get back to you.

Give Me the Simple Life

Friends in the States ask me what it would cost "to live a simple life" here. I am not sure I can judge what they mean by "simple." Just as one man's treasure is another man's trash, one person's simple is another's luxury. Actually, my own idea of simple is pretty nebulous. Mainly, it is not accumulating a lot of "stuff." Except maybe, books. It's not being a big-time consumer, and being concerned enough about the environment not to pollute it any more than I can help, by recycling. Recycling not only helps to live simply, it helps to live more cheaply. I live, for the most part, on products that are available in Costa Rica. But not entirely. I am delighted when some new product from the U.S. or Europe comes into the supermarket. But I rationalize that it is the global economy.

However, there are people living here who have built simple homes near a rainforest or in a small town, far from San José, who really live a simple life. They grow their own organic crops, make their own bread, and survive very nicely without TV or telephone – or even electricity. I could not do that.

My idea of simple includes going out to dinner – sometimes at friends' homes and sometimes at restaurants. This past week was a surfeit of delicious meals. First came a dinner party – most of us actually have dinner now in the middle of the day – at Joan and Lenny's where a multiple-course Moroccan feast was served. My favorite courses were the lamb stew and Turkish coffee. I didn't think I would eat again for at least three days, but that evening we had our traditional *Perros Calientes* supper at Sandy's. The sad fact seems to be that the more you eat, the more you can eat. Hot dogs and baked beans never tasted so good.

On Saturday Sandy, Anabel and I celebrated the Chinese New Year at the special dinner (in the middle of the day) at Tin Jo's Asian restaurant. Maria and Roberto, the owners, had prepared a really comfortable and fun buffet-style dinner of a variety of very good Chinese dishes. They also had a dragon dancer to entertain us. There were lessons in a number of things, including origami and the use of chopsticks. They even had special activities for the children. At the table next to us was a little boy of about three, maybe four. I love little boys at that age. Little girls already seem wise about the ways of the world and how to manipulate it. Little boys don't have a clue. This little boy was wandering from his table looking quite at sea about what was going on. A bit later a dragon dance of children had formed and was parading through the restaurant. The front child had a lion's mask and the children behind were holding on to a long red canopy or each other – much like a conga line. As they passed by our table we saw the little lost boy in the line, his head thrown back, and an expression of pure joy on his face as he passed his table, as if to say, "Look, Mom, I'm dancing!" The three of us burst out laughing with him.

Again I thought I couldn't eat a thing for days, but that night I was hungry again!

So living the simple life according to Stuart sometimes seems pretty luxurious even to me. And we come to the most important part of living in Costa Rica. Simple or complicated, a life well lived needs friends. And for whatever reason – I think partly because just the fact of having moved here pre-selects the people whom one is apt to meet – it seems easier to come upon people you really like here.

Of Time and Money, and Spending Both in Costa Rica

I am often asked, "Now that you are retired and living in Costa Rica, just what do you do all day?"

Sometimes I hem and I haw, and then I say, "Well, you see, there are two kinds of people in the world. There are people who have more money than time, and then there are people who have more time than money. People with more money spend their money saving time, and people with more time spend their time saving money. Of course," I add, "The idle rich and the working poor, by definition, don't fit in this division."

Then I explain that I have always been a member of the second group. With more time than money, I don't send my clothes to the laundry or even the dry cleaners. It is amazing how many garments marked "dry clean only" wash well. Years ago, I learned from some one else's maid in Majorca who was washing her Señor's herringbone tweed jacket that the secret was not to "shock" the material with either too hot or too cold water. Speaking of washing clothes, I don't have a clothes dryer. I hang all of my clothes on lines in my *pila* (my open-air laundry room). I don't have a full-time maid and I don't use convenience foods. I usually cook everything from scratch. All of these things and cooking from scratch take time.

I have this wonderful little washing machine that I call my "high participation washer." I have to fill and empty the water via the faucet, and transfer the clothing to the spinner by hand. The clothes spinner makes hanging clothes very easy because they are almost dry. I wouldn't use a clothes dryer if you gave me one – it ruins more clothes and costs a lot doing it. Besides, I love the feel of sheets and towels that have been line-dried. Towels dried on the line have some body to them and are good for the circulation.

Still explaining, I go on, "When I shop, I comparison-shop." This takes time and sometimes, as my friends with money like to point out, I have saved only a few colones. When I was married and living in Majorca, my husband hated shopping with me in Palma until one day he had an epiphany and from then on trailed happily after me. He said he realized that walking around town, shopping and window shopping, and being among the milling throng of people, was part of living, too.

I smile and continue, "As a money saver, of course, I believe in recycling." (I am waiting for *Cosas Americanas* stores that will sell household items, to join the *Ropa Americana* stores.) "And I don't throw anything away until I am sure I can't find another use for it." Those strawberry baskets make great mini-garbage holders for the mini sinks they have here. And they are nice little organizers for lipsticks and things in the bathroom. At this point, I spare the questioner more of my clever recycling ideas.

"With more time than money," I continue, "I don't have a car (the biggest money gobbling time-saver of all) to go somewhere. I walk, or take the bus, and sometimes a taxi. Taxis are very reasonable here.

"Walking, I notice things like new stores that have opened or replaced old stores. (The store where I bought my bamboo furniture now does tattooing and body-piercing.) I stop to read *ejecutivos* – luncheon specials – on the menus posted outside modest but promising looking new restaurants. I stop to gaze at new buildings that have just gone up and stand for a moment in front of a newly excavated hole, trying to remember what was there just a week ago."

I pause for just a moment and add, "A time-saving person, I think, is often a specialist, whereas to be a money-saving person you have to be a generalist." Then I notice that the person who asked me what I do with my time has become glassy-eyed and has quite forgotten what the question was, so I say,

"Well, the short answer is, it takes all day for me to live in Costa Rica."

Unexpected Gifts

When they retire, most people probably are able to involve themselves in a hobby they have long had (like growing roses or repairing furniture). But I have never been a hobby person.

The only hobby I ever had was making up double-crostics, which I call Litacrostics, a type of word puzzle few people have ever heard of and even fewer ever want to solve. Given free time, I am a game player – especially games such as Charades, Scrabble and Trivial Pursuit. Reading is such an important part of my life; I don't consider it a pastime.

One of the surprising rewards of living in Costa Rica is being able to return to the things I loved doing years ago – such as writing a column for a newspaper and acting, both of which I did when I was in college. Off and on through the years, I have acted in little theater groups (and once was part owner of a legitimate theater in Hollywood), and I have written for newsletters and even a health column for women. But all of that was many years ago. I didn't expect to get back to these things when I retired.

I moved to Costa Rica pretty much the way I have made any of my past 50 or so moves: I threw myself into the new pond to see if I could swim. Once here, recovering from job burnout and becoming adjusted to a new culture, making new friends and getting settled took time and energy, but when I finally lifted my nose above water, I realized I could act (not in the theater sense) instead of react.

Making friends in Costa Rica has been easier than in any of the places I have lived before, in part because the foreigners who live here are already pre-selected. We all have in common the desire and willingness to try a new culture, to venture into a bit of the unknown. And then, because Costa Rica is really a small town, you dare to try something that might have intimidated you in your own country. I dared to audition for the part of Grandma Prudence in a radio *novela* aimed at teaching children in the *campo* English. When they called to tell me I had the part I was sure they had made a mistake. Yet my dream of acting on radio had actually come true.

I had the good luck to work with the cast and crew of *Ten Little Indians,* a Little Theater Group production. Our ages ranged from 17 to 74, and we were a wonderfully compatible group. We came from at least five countries, including Costa Rica. Most of us had lived in more than one country, in places as far-flung as the Canadian Arctic, New Zealand and Africa. Everyone seemed to have lived singularly interesting lives. Yet those of us who were retired agreed that this was the best time of our lives. This has given me something to think about lately. Although being retired is a happy condition in itself, living in Costa Rica has a great deal to do with our sense of well-being.

I've been thinking about what I have here: a beautiful and peaceful country unlikely to be threatened by another world power, large or small, a host country whose citizens are gracious and charming, a climate that requires no air conditioning or heating, a great variety of good food at reasonable prices. These are all conditions that contribute to the good life.

Having solved the problem of bureaucratic red tape and other frustrations by simply not owning anything except essentials, I am generally not hassled by the minutiae of living. Here, I am free of the subtle and not-so-subtle pressures to be a consumer. (I am eternally grateful that no Fifth Avenue window dresser has come here to work magic on window displays in San José.) I have the time and opportunity to make and enjoy friends. How does that song go? "I've got the sun in the morning and the moon at night." If I want to, in one day I can watch the sun dawn over the Atlantic and watch it sink into the Pacific at sunset. Yes, it is very easy to be content in Costa Rica.

Jo Stuart has acted, taught, written and lived in many parts of the western world, including Majorca, Brazil, New York and California. She makes her permanent home in Costa Rica, where her newspaper columns celebrate the good life.

Made in the USA
San Bernardino, CA
08 March 2016